The
Fast Forward
MBA in Business
Planning
for Growth

THE FAST FORWARD MBA SERIES

The Fast Forward MBA Series provides time-pressed business professionals and students with concise, one-stop information to help them solve business problems and make smart, informed business decisions. All of the volumes, written by industry leaders, contain "tough ideas made easy." The published books in this series are:

The Fast Forward MBA in Business Communication
(0-471-32731-x)
by Lauren Vicker & Ron Hein

The Fast Forward MBA in Project Management
(0-471-32546-5)
by Eric Verzuh

The Fast Forward MBA in Negotiating and Dealmaking
(0-471-25698-6)
by Roy J. Lewicki and Alexander Hiam

The Fast Forward MBA in Financial Planning
(0-471-23829-5)
by Ed McCarthy

The Fast Forward MBA in Hiring
(0-471-24212-8)
by Max Messmer

The Fast Forward MBA in Investing
(0-471-24661-1)
by John Waggoner

The Fast Forward MBA in Technology Management
(0-471-23980-1)
by Daniel J. Petrozzo

The Fast Forward MBA Pocket Reference
(0-471-14595-5)
by Paul A. Argenti

The Fast Forward MBA in Marketing
(0-471-16616-2)
by Dallas Murphy

The Fast Forward MBA in Business
(0-471-14660-9)
by Virginia O'Brien

The Fast Forward MBA in Finance
(0-471-10930-4)
by John Tracy

The Fast Forward MBA in Business Planning for Growth

PHILIP WALCOFF

John Wiley & Sons, Inc.

New York • Chichester • Weinheim • Brisbane • Singapore • Toronto

Published by John Wiley & Sons, Inc.
Published simultaneously in Canada.

This publication is designed to provide accurate and authoritative
information in regard to the subject matter covered. It is sold
with the understanding that the publisher is not engaged in
rendering professional services. If legal, accounting, medical,
psychological or any other expert assistance is required, the
services of a competent professional person should be sought.

Library of Congress Cataloging-in-Publication Data:
Walcoff, Philip.
    The fast forward MBA in business planning for growth /
Philip Walcoff.
        p.   cm. — (The fast forward MBA series)
    Includes index.
    ISBN 0-471-34548-2 (pbk. : alk. paper)
    1. Business planning.   2. Strategic planning   3. Industrial
management.   4. Industrial organization.   I. Title.   II. Series.
HD30.28.W3348   1999
658.4′012—dc21   99-21723
                                                                        CIP

Printed in the United States of America.

10 9 8 7 6 5 4 3 2 1

*This book is dedicated to Albert Nelson,
my life-long friend and coach,
and a person who unselfishly shared,
with me and many others,
his knowledge and experience,
his excitement,
and his love of just "doing business."*

Philip Walcoff is the cofounder of a high-technology information system company that grew from 2 employees in 1982 to more than 600 employees in 1990 with more than $60 million in sales. Currently, he is President of PWI Business Solutions, where he brings his experience and expertise to large and small companies in developing and implementing action-oriented plans for growth. He has written for such publications as Washington Technology's *Small Business Report* and the *Columbia Business Monthly*. He has been featured in *Warfield's Business Record* and the *Baltimore Business Journal* and is a frequent speaker on business planning. He lives in Maryland.

ACKNOWLEDGMENTS

To Peter Michael Kelly, who first provided me the opportunity to become a businessman; to Richard J. Otero, my former partner and associate throughout my career, who whetted my appetite for entrepreneuring; to Howard Weinberg, my friend, associate, and sounding board; and to Preston Bruce Jr. and Joseph Kolthoff, my lifelong friends. To all my clients, who have been my teachers and my listeners and who have provided me the opportunity to support them in applying my business-planning process in pursuit of attaining their visions of their companies. Special thanks to Sandi Patty, Pete DeNucci, and my editor, Renana Meyers, for reviewing the draft document and making it a better product. Finally, to my wife Gwyn, my children, Jill and Jonathan, Jeff, and Lisa and Morten, my sister Eve, and my brother Hal, who have been my greatest supporters.

CONTENTS

If I always appear prepared, it is because before embarking on an undertaking, I have meditated for long and have foreseen what might occur. It is not genius which reveals to me suddenly and secretly what I should do in circumstances unexpected by others; it is thought and meditation.

—*Napoleon Bonaparte*

So, what's your plan? If you haven't, like Napoleon, "thought and meditated" about your business future and, most important, written it down, this book will go a long way in helping you develop and implement an effective, action-oriented, business plan. In the near term, this plan will get you focused to enable the growth and success of your company or organization; in the long term, it will assist you in developing your business into the company you dream about. Almost all books on business planning provide guidance on the preparation of a document, the sole purpose of which is to raise capital for a business venture. If that is your intent, put this book back on the shelf and try the ones to the left or right—I'm certain they will address your need. *This* book is focused on *developing the strategies and supporting tactics to grow your company or organization,* on *bringing more to the bottom line,* and on *making the workplace a more enjoyable and exciting place to be for you and your employees.*

As the owner (or potential owner) or manager of a business, you are most likely in one of these three situations:

1. *You have an idea for a business,* but you need some guidance as to how to get started.

2. *Your company or organization is not growing,* and you need to gain focus and develop and implement a strategy that puts you on a growth path.

3. *Your company or organization is growing,* but lacks focus, a direction, or a strategy for continued, controlled growth.

Whichever situation you are in, you should undertake the following:

- Develop an action-oriented business plan with strategies and supporting tactics that foster the growth of your company or organization.

- Implement a process to manage this plan to success.

Based on the points I have made concerning growth and considering the title of this book, *Business Planning for Growth,* it should be apparent that this focus will be on growing your company. I believe every business owner or manager should view growth as a critical element of success. You may ask, why is growth so important? In their book, *Action Plans for the Small Business,* Vyakarnam and Lepperd[1] point out that a company's business base is like a bucket that must be kept filled to a certain level with incoming business to achieve ongoing success. If the company surpasses this level, it faces a rosy future. If it doesn't, failure is just around the corner.

They go on to say that most businesses are like *leaky* buckets, because customers relocate, switch to a competitor, or stop doing business with you for a host of other reasons. Therefore, in order to keep business at the same level, companies must keep up a steady level of growth. Vyakarnam and Lepperd conclude that "growth is tantamount to survival."

My experience has been that most business owners and managers don't want to keep business at the same level. Entrepreneurs want to increase sales, enter new markets, and expand products and services—they see growth as a major reason for being in business. In addition to "keeping the leaky bucket filled," they realize that growth offers the possibility of greater corporate stability and increased profits and company value. There are less tangible but equally appealing reasons for growth. Having been part of growing a company from my partner and me to 600 employees in 5 major locations within the span of 8 short years, I can say that growth is a most rewarding professional experience. Being part of a company on the move provides a great feeling of achievement in meeting life's challenges and truly making something of your professional life.

In today's highly competitive and volatile business environment, it is critical that companies develop and implement effective business plans and supporting processes to ensure future growth and success. Although about a million companies are started each year, an equal number are closing. One of the major reasons cited for this high rate of failure is lack of planning. Failure aside, if you don't plan, you will be outperformed by companies that do use planning as an important element in their approach to conducting business.

This book is written for business owners and managers who want to gain focus and grow their companies or organizations and make them more successful. Its applicability ranges from one-person start-up companies to very large businesses employing thousands of people. It is also applicable to managers of government and nonprofit organizations who don't have the profit (or perhaps growth) incentives but wish to gain focus and direction for their organizations. It makes a powerful case for the importance of a documented business plan, presents by way of a series of exercises a straightforward approach to preparing the plan, and describes the actions necessary to manage the plan to success.

Of key importance is that this book presents a unique approach to planning based on actual experiences I have gained over my 35-year business career. As mentioned earlier, this experience includes cofounding a home-based business in 1982 and growing it into a highly successful 600-person high-technology company with offices throughout the eastern United

States. Since 1990, I have been working as a consultant with over 70 companies of all types and sizes, identifying and dealing with the major issues facing companies today and supporting their development of action-oriented business plans that foster growth and profitability. This book captures and employs the essence of these experiences first-hand.

The planning approach I use is not that of the "standard business plan," which focuses on raising capital, or the "strategic plan," which is woefully short on tactics and most often sits on a shelf gathering dust. Instead, it is an approach that focuses on growing your business, bringing more to the bottom line, and designing a company or organization that is efficient, effective, and enjoyable.

More than a tutorial, this is a hands-on workbook that will guide you, step by step, through the process of preparing your business plan. Completing the exercises in this book will result in your having a working business plan in hand, as well as a process for managing it to success. As a result, you will be on your way to making the vision of your company or organization a reality. I heartily wish you success.

The
Fast Forward
MBA in Business
Planning
for Growth

1

The Business-Planning Process
Three Steps to an Effective Business Plan

Those who fail to plan, plan to fail.
—George Hewell

This part on the business-planning process presents two chapters that provide an introduction to business plans and an overview of the business-planning process that you will use to develop your business plan.

Chapter 1: An Introduction to Business Plans answers the question, "Why do I need a business plan?" It also describes the two most popular kinds of plans found in today's business world and explains why they generally fail to meet the objectives of the developers.

Chapter 2: The Three-Step Planning Process presents an introduction to the three steps you will use to develop and manage your own business plan—identifying the issues, developing the plan, and managing the plan. Performing these three steps avoids the planning pitfalls described in Chapter 1, thereby helping you successfully achieve your planning objectives.

CHAPTER 1

An Introduction to Business Plans

plan (plan) n. [Fr., plan, plane, foundation: . . .] refers to any detailed method, formulated beforehand, for doing or making something . . .
—*Webster's New World Dictionary* [1]

Keeping this definition in mind, what do a housing developer, a professional football coach, a military commander, and a commercial airline pilot have in common? The answer is that they all begin their projects with a written plan. These construction plans, game plans, battle plans, and flight plans (and business plans as well) all have something in common—the objectives and approach to accomplishing the mission of each is determined and documented *prior* to undertaking the mission. Referring to this part's opening quote, these planners *don't* plan on failing.

BUSINESS CHARACTERIZATION BY SIZE

The U.S. Small Business Administration (SBA) reports that more than 22 million businesses filed tax returns in 1995.[2] As shown in Figure 1.1, the large majority of these businesses (approximately 17 million) were sole-proprietorships (no employees), about a third (approximately 5 million) had from 1 to 500 employees, and only 15,000 businesses had more than 500 employees. The SBA defines a small business as a company that has fewer than 500 employees.[3]

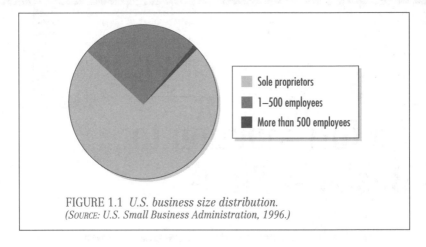

FIGURE 1.1 *U.S. business size distribution.*
(*SOURCE: U.S. Small Business Administration, 1996.*)

When considering the planning process, I prefer to define a small business as a company that is typically striving to achieve growth and stability. It has a small management team most often consisting of the owner and perhaps one or two other managers, is usually doing less than $1 million in annual sales, and employs 1 to 15 people. In contrast, I view a medium-sized firm as having a management team (infrastructure) in place and diversifying and gaining maturity. These companies are seeking continued growth and increased profitability, are doing between $10 million and $50 million in sales, and employ up to 500 people. Companies between $1 million and $10 million are typically in transition from being owner controlled and managed to building a management infrastructure. They can be considered small or medium-sized depending on how quickly they are making the transition to shared management.

In terms of business planning, my experience has shown that the small firm almost always relies on its president to develop and implement the business plan, whereas the medium-sized firm typically involves a management team in the development and implementation of its business plan.

KEY CONCEPT — MOST COMPANIES DON'T PLAN

Over the last 8 years, I have worked with more than 70 small to medium-sized companies (most of them having less than 500 employees), ranging from start-ups to companies earning $400 million in gross sales. I have helped them make something of their companies through the development and implementation of action-oriented business plans. In my capacity as a business consultant, it has become clear to me that most owners of small to medium-sized companies or organizations *do not* have documented business plans—and, further, see little value in them. And as for the small number of companies or organizations that do develop plans, they typically do not *implement* them.

Chances are, you are in the majority of businesses that don't plan, or that plan but don't implement their plans. Their owners and managers see the planning efforts of the housing developer, the football coach, the military commander, the airline pilot, and others as special cases that are, therefore, not applicable to their businesses. Notice that large companies are not included in my reference to nonplanners, and this should tell you something—a business doesn't *become* large or *stay* large without *planning.* I'm not suggesting that every successful company started off with a business plan, but I can say that, by far, the majority either succeeded because they had a documented business plan in their early history, or they developed one along the way and have it in place today.

(At this point, I want to note that I understand that readers most likely either own or manage a business, manage an element of a business, or are considering going into a business. In the interest of brevity, when I use the term *business owner,* understand that my remarks apply as well to business managers, managers of business elements, and would-be owners and managers.)

 **BUSINESS FAILURES ARE LINKED TO LACK OF PLANNING**

The U.S. Small Business Administration reports that although almost 1 million new businesses are started each year, almost as many close their doors each year.[4] Figure 1.2 reflects the SBA's data on the failure rate of businesses over a 10-year period. As indicated, almost a quarter of all businesses fail in the first 2 years, over half after 5 years, and almost 80 percent after 10 years.

Some books on business present even more dismal numbers. Joseph R. Mancuso, one of the most popular authors of how-to books for small businesses, states in his book *How to Write a Winning Business Plan* that "over half of new businesses fail within the first two years of operation—over 90 percent fail within the first ten years. A major reason for failure is lack of planning. The best way to enhance your chances of success is to plan and follow through on your planning."[5] Corello and Hazelgren state in their book *The Complete Book of Business Plans* that "about 1 million businesses per year are started and 80% fail in 5 years."[6]

In his *Small Business Start-Up Guide,* Dr. Robert Sullivan cites planning as one of nine steps to business success. He states, "A major reason for business failure is lack of planning. Prepare a strategic plan for your business that clearly defines your mission, your present situation, your strategies, and where you want to be in the next three to five years. This plan will be your roadmap to effective decision making."[7] These failure statistics strongly support George

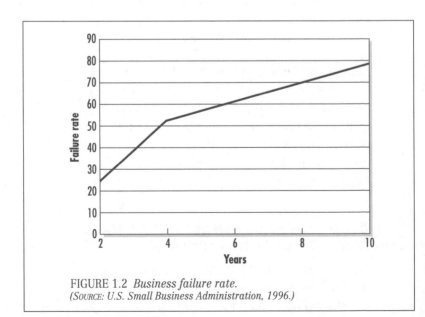

FIGURE 1.2 *Business failure rate.*
(Source: U.S. Small Business Administration, 1996.)

Hewell's statement cited at the beginning of this part: "Those who fail to plan, plan to fail."

Many a maxim links success to planning:

- On any journey, we must find out where we are before we can plan the first step.—*Kathy Boevink*
- Nothing Happens Unless First a Dream—*Carl Sandburg*
- The future belongs to those who plan for it.—*Anonymous*
- The end justifies the means.—*H. Busenbaum* (c. 1650)
- If you don't know where you are going, how can you expect to get there?—*Basil S. Walsh*
- Even if you are on the right track, you'll get run over if you just sit there.—*Will Rogers*
- Goals determine what you're going to be.—*Julius Erving*
- The very essence of leadership is that you have to have a vision. You can't blow an uncertain trumpet.—*Thomas Hesburgh*
- Begin with the end in mind.—*Stephen Covey's* Habit #2 of highly effective people

Referring to the last bullet, Steven Covey says in his popular book *The 7 Habits of Highly Effective People*," "The extent to which you begin with the end in mind often determines whether or not you are able to create a successful enterprise. Most business failures begin in the first creation, with problems such as undercapitalization, misunderstanding of the market, or *lack of a business plan.*"[8]

 **REASONS WHY COMPANIES DON'T PLAN**

Even though we may agree with the value of business planning, most of us still avoid it. Several key reasons are the following:

- I don't have the time.
- I don't know where to begin.
- I don't know who can help.
- It's too expensive to hire a planning expert.
- I don't need a plan; I know what I need to do.

Another reason that I suspect is a major stumbling block is that it's not threatening to carry a business plan around in your head. But once you've put it on paper, you're committed to it—accountable both to your staff and to yourself. That makes many of us very uncomfortable, and so we opt to shy away from the documented business-planning process.

 **WHY YOU NEED A BUSINESS PLAN**

Writing this book stems from my desire to get a message to business owners and managers that answers the question, "Why do you need a business plan?" My answer is that to increase the odds of developing and maintaining a successful business, you must:

1. Understand the internal issues in the way of your success.

2. Define and document the necessary strategies and supporting tactics (the business plan) to address these issues, grow, and be more successful.

3. Implement a process in the company to effectively manage the plan to success.

You need a business plan because it is a critically important element of running a business. Without it, you increase the risk of becoming a business-failure statistic.

 **TYPES OF BUSINESS PLANS**

When you think *business plan,* what comes to your mind? A number of different types of plans are found in today's business world. Two very popular plans, with which you likely have some familiarity, are what I call the *classic business plan* and the *strategic plan.* The *classic business plan* is the one that you will most often be referred to at your local bookstore or library when you ask for a book on business planning. The *strategic plan* is the one that always looks and reads like a doctoral thesis and collects dust on bookshelves. Let's examine these two types of plans in more detail.

The Classic Business Plan

The classic business plan typically presents a description of the company; an analysis of the industry and the particular markets it's in; a description of the competition; a marketing plan; and a description of the operations, management, and organization of the company, as well as its financials, including an income statement, a balance sheet, and a cash-flow analysis. This plan describes the history of the company, its current position, and projections for its future. Its main purpose is to raise capital from outside sources or to persuade senior management to invest in a particular organization or concept. It's not really a plan but more a statement as to the worthiness of the business venture—a selling document. It's somewhat short on strategy and doesn't address tactics at all. These types of plans are necessary if you are seeking to raise capital, and I have already cited several books on classic business plans in this chapter.

In his book on business planning, *How to Create a Successful Business Plan,* David E. Gumpert defines a business plan as "a document that convincingly demonstrates that your business can sell enough of its product or service to make a satisfactory profit and be attractive to potential backers."[9] I contend that this classical business plan is not really a plan at all, but a statement as to the worthiness of a business venture in an effort to raise capital. As Gumpert goes on to say, it's a selling document.

The Strategic Plan

On the other hand, the strategic plan is long on strategy but, like the classic business plan, it doesn't address the critical tactics for making the plan a reality. Typically prepared once a year, the strategic plan contains a description of the company and its market, and strategies for attacking this market, as well as a set of long-range goals, usually covering a five-year period. The problem here is that once they are completed, these strategic plans, often bound in attractive three-ring binders, are typically placed on the shelf and are never referred to again until about two weeks prior to the next year's strategic planning session. The reason they sit on the shelf gathering dust is that they focus on long-range activities and don't relate to the day-to-day tactical activities associated with acquiring business and growing a company.

KEY CONCEPT STRATEGY AND TACTICS

At this point it's important to distinguish *strategy* from *tactics*. Webster defines strategy and tactics as follows:

> strategy n. [Fr., stratégie . . .] a stratagem or artful means to some end . . .

> tactics n. [Gr., taktika . . .] any methods used to gain an end . . .[10]

In terms of business planning, I view *strategy* as a road map and *tactics* as the vehicle to implement the strategy. I also view strategy as taking place in the long-term, whereas tactics is more a short-term undertaking. With these definitions in mind, strategic plans are just the road maps without the tactics.

OTHER TYPES OF PLANS USED IN BUSINESS

Other types of business plans are used in the corporate domain, including manufacturing plans, financial plans, staffing plans, facilities plans, communications plans, and marketing plans. These types of plans are typically short-termed and necessarily are focused on a particular segment of the company's operation. I don't diminish the importance of these types of plans, but they do not address the broad issues of successfully growing the company and will not be further addressed here.

K E Y
CONCEPT **WHY BUSINESS PLANS FAIL**

As discussed earlier, the majority of those companies that develop plans fail to implement them. In taking on the business-planning process it is important to understand the four most common reasons for this failure:

1. *The plan doesn't account for roadblocks.* Every company, including yours, has its set of issues that are significant roadblocks to successfully implementing a business plan. Without a doubt, these issues impede your business' growth and success. These roadblocks or issues generally appear in nine major arenas:

   - Ineffective *marketing and sales* to sustain and grow the company
   - *Personnel and compensation* problems, affecting the hiring and retaining of employees
   - Ineffective *communications* up, down, and across the line, resulting in inefficiency and a stressful work environment
   - Lack of sufficient *systems and processes* to support effective operations of the company
   - Problems in the *management and operations* of the company, affecting the future health of the business and its employees
   - *Cultural* problems, affecting every element of the company
   - Poor *planning* or ineffective *plan implementation*
   - Insufficient *resources,* including staff, space, equipment, and other facilities
   - Problems dealing with the company's *finances and administration*

   These issues, which will be discussed more thoroughly in Part 2, demand serious attention and must be addressed in your business plan in order to remove the barriers to its successful implementation. Defining and dealing with these issues will allow you to get on with growing your company, making it more profitable, and creating a workplace that is more enjoyable for you and your employees.

2. *The plan is too limited in scope.*   As dis-cussed earlier, the *classical business plan* is focused on raising money and does not ade-quately address strategies and tactics for growing a company. On the other hand, *strategic plans* typically focus on marketing and sales strategies to the exclusion of other elements of the company. These plans lack the necessary tactics for successful imple-mentation. Part 3 presents a format to develop your business plan. This format addresses all components of the company (not just marketing and sales) and encom-passes both the strategies and the supporting tactics necessary to make your plan a living document—a tool for managing the growth and success of your company.

3. *There is no management process in place to support plan implementation.*   Once the plan is developed, you need to implement a process for managing the plan to success. You cannot put the plan on the shelf and expect success at the end of the year—the plan needs regular attention throughout the year. You must hold yourself accountable to take the steps necessary to implement your plan. In larger companies, the senior staff members will take on the responsibility to implement various portions of the plan. It's up to you to hold your managers accountable for achieving those objectives they take on. In addition, regular reviews of the progress toward attaining the plan's objectives must take place. Part 4 presents the process for managing your plan to success.

4. *The plan action items lack priority.*   The necessary tactical actions to be taken to implement the plan usually take a back seat to the pressing demands of day-to-day busi-ness. Most senior managers view planning actions (e.g., getting that new accounting sys-tem in place or developing that new market-ing brochure) as just one more set of things to do. They believe that these action items can be put off until next week, next month, or when things "lighten up." A discussion of

committing to the plan's implementation is presented in Part 4.

PLAN OR DIE

Many of the fires that senior management continuously fights stem from the issues or roadblocks (as introduced in item 1 in the preceding section) that abound in most companies. If these issues were identified and strategies and tactics were developed to address and eventually eliminate them, senior managers would have more time to devote to growing their company and making it more successful. In *Plan or Die!*, Nolan, Goodstein, and Pfeiffer point out that "strategic planning and strategic management (the day-to-day implementation of the strategic plan) are the two most important, never-ending jobs of management, especially top management."[11]

STEPHEN COVEY'S TIME MANAGEMENT MATRIX

In *The 7 Habits of Highly Effective People*, Stephen Covey developed the time management matrix presented in Figure 1.3. This matrix shows that managers spend their time in four different quadrants—performing activities that are (1) urgent and important, (2) urgent but not important, (3) not urgent but important, and (4) not urgent and not important.[12]

Covey points out that *urgent* means something requiring immediate attention—such as a ring-

Urgent Important	Not urgent Important
Urgent Not important	Not urgent Not important

FIGURE 1.3 *Covey's time management matrix.*
(*SOURCE: The 7 Habits of Highly Effective People, by Stephen R. Covey; 1990, Simon & Schuster.*)

ing telephone. On the other hand, something *important* deals with results, such as your values, your mission, and your goals—your *plan.* The *urgent and important* quadrant (top left) reflects crisis management. Covey says that we all have some crises in our lives, but this quadrant consumes many people who are problem solvers and deadline driven. Many people prefer spending time in this quadrant because they like doing *important* (also what they think are urgent) things. According to Covey, "That's how people who manage their lives by crisis live."

Then there are those who spend large parts of their time in the *urgent and not important* quadrant (lower left), thinking they're actually in the urgent and important quadrant. They react to urgent situations thinking that they are important, but Covey says that "the urgency of these matters is often based on the priorities and expectations of others."[13]

Covey points out that the *not urgent and important* quadrant (upper right) "is the heart of personal management." He goes on to say that "effective people stay out of the Urgent and Not Important quadrant (lower left) and the Not Urgent and Not Important quadrant (lower right), urgent or not, they aren't important." This last point is critical. By putting effort into the planning arena (the not urgent and important quadrant) through identifying issues and developing strategies and tactics to eliminate them, you will, as Covey says, be able to "shrink the Urgent and Important quadrant down to size by spending more time in the Not Urgent and Important quadrant." Implementing your business plan is where you perform *important but not urgent* activities.

OBJECTIVES OF THIS BOOK

Because business planning is a critical element in ensuring the success of any business, and because most business owners and managers don't do it, I have written this book with the following three objectives in mind:

1. To provide you with an understanding of effective business-planning and plan-implementation techniques

2. To provide a straightforward and comprehensive approach to documenting a business plan for your enterprise

3. To prepare you to conduct a planning session in your own company or organization that will enroll others in the plan

With your company's plan in hand and the knowledge of how to successfully implement it, you'll be able to move forward with an effective tool for surviving and growing in today's challenging business environment.

END POINT

Most companies don't plan, and of those that do, most don't implement their plans. The two most popular business plans are the *classic business plan* and the *strategic business plan,* and both have serious drawbacks with regard to supporting the growth and success of your company.

Business plans are not successfully implemented for four key reasons:

1. The roadblocks to plan implementation aren't identified and acted upon.

2. The plan is too limited in scope (focused on raising capital or limited to developing marketing strategies).

3. The company has no plan-management process in place.

4. The plan's action items lack priority.

With this in mind, let's move to Chapter 2, which presents a business planning process that counters these four reasons for plan failures and forms the basis for the remainder of the book.

The Three-Step Planning Process

The hardest thing to learn in life is which bridge to cross and which to burn.
—Laurence J. Peter

KEY CONCEPT — A THREE-STEP PROCESS

The three-step planning process that is the cornerstone of a successful business plan is pictured in Figure 2.1. This process includes (1) identifying the issues or roadblocks, (2) developing the plan, and (3) managing the plan. These three critical steps provide the necessary ingredients to develop and implement your business plan effectively and to obtain the desired results from your planning efforts.

Identify the Issues

The first step of the planning process is to *identify the major issues* (or roadblocks) facing your company in its move toward increased growth and profitability. These issues, introduced in Chapter 1 and described in more detail in Part 2, must be addressed in order to remove the barriers to successfully implementing the business plan. These issues may include a haphazard and uncoordinated approach to business development, a lack of programs for rewarding and training employees, a lack of management accountability and authority, significant communications gaps throughout the company, and

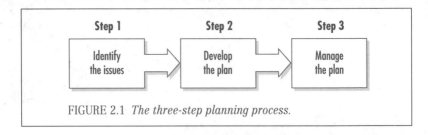

FIGURE 2.1 *The three-step planning process.*

a host of others, as described in Part 2. The business plan is an excellent vehicle for developing the necessary strategies and tactics to address these issues. Including these issue-driven tactical actions in your business plan will go a long way toward supporting your plan's implementation.

Develop the Plan

The second step of the planning process is to *develop the plan.* This involves the integration of strategic (long-term) and tactical (short-term) elements into a single plan that addresses questions ranging from what business you want to be in (strategy) to who will make what sales call next week (tactics). Defining and managing to completion the tactical actions in support of the strategy is what makes the business-planning process effective. The plan becomes a living document, in contrast to the plan that sits on the shelf gathering dust. The detailed process for developing a business plan is addressed in Part 3.

If you own or manage a small company with one or more employees whom you feel are important to the future of the company, or you head a larger company with a management team in place, I strongly suggest that you hold a planning session of your own to involve these employees in the process. This will enhance your plan and allow those key staff members to buy into it. Chapter 11 provides guidelines for holding this planning session with your staff.

Manage the Plan

The third step of the planning process is to *manage the plan.* The first two steps—identifying issues and developing the plan—are relatively straightforward and can be accomplished in a week or two. However, managing the plan requires a dedicated effort throughout the year. Recall from Chapter 1 that the majority of companies that develop plans don't implement them. Managing the plan requires continuous discipline, including taking the time to review your progress and keep the plan's objectives on track. It's about holding you and others accountable for achieving results.

Recall from Chapter 1 Covey's remarks about management's responsibility to do the *important* things, and Nolan, Goodstein, and Pfeiffer's emphatic statement that senior management's primary responsibility is to implement the business plan. On any business day, accomplishing some small step toward achieving a plan objective won't be viewed as urgent, but it is very important for meeting your short-term objectives and eventually your long-term goal— implementing your business plan.

The planning approach illustrated in Figure 2.1 goes beyond simply developing a document. It encompasses the implementation of a process within the company for *managing* the plan to success through regularly scheduled progress reviews and for incorporating the plan's action items into management's day-to-day business activities. The plan itself is not enough—you need to implement a process for identifying who is accountable for achieving certain results and managing the plan in order to monitor performance and make any necessary midcourse corrections. Remember, you can't prepare a plan, put it on a shelf, and expect success at the end of the year. The plan requires regular attention throughout the year. A more detailed discussion of plan management is presented in Part 4.

What distinguishes the proven three-step planning approach from that of the familiar classic or strategic business plans mentioned earlier is as follows:

1. Issues or roadblocks to the plan's implementation are identified and incorporated into the planning process.

2. The plan is broad in scope, incorporating both strategic and tactical elements, and it addresses all components of the company (marketing and sales, operations, finance, accounting, human resources, and administration).

3. The approach encompasses a management process to support the plan's implementation.

END POINT

The three-step planning process incorporates identifying issues, developing the plan, and managing the plan to success. Performing these three activities puts you in an excellent position to make the vision you have of your organization a reality. The remainder of this book will take you through each of the three critical planning steps. Upon completion of this book and its associated exercises, you will have a business plan for your company in hand and an understanding of the process for managing the plan to success. Referring to the quote by Peter at the beginning of this chapter, performing the three-step planning process will shed considerable light on "which bridge to cross and which to burn."

Identify the Issues

On any journey, we must find out where we are before we can plan the first step.
—*Kathy Boevink*

Step 1	Step 2	Step 3
Identify the issues	Develop the plan	Manage the plan

This part describes step 1 of the planning process—identifying the issues—or in Kathy Boevink's terminology, finding out where you are. Chapters 3, 4, and 5 cover popular function-specific and companywide issues, along with appropriate issue response options. Part 3 covers defining actions for dealing with these issues.

Chapter 3: Issues in the Way of Success presents an approach for gathering the major issues facing companies and, in order to help you clearly understand what part of your organization needs to take on the task of dealing with these issues, categorizes them as either function-specific or companywide.

Chapter 4: Function-Specific Issues and Appropriate Response Options presents the major issues in the four functional areas of marketing and sales, personnel and compensation, management and operations, and finance and administration and offers approaches for resolving them. A series of examples and exercises is also included to help you identify your own function-specific issues and develop appropriate responses.

Chapter 5: Companywide Issues and Appropriate Response Options presents the five major issue categories in the five enterprisewide areas of communications, culture, systems and processes, planning, and resources. Again, a series of examples and exercises is included to help you identify your own companywide issues and develop approaches to eliminate these issues.

Issues in the Way of Success

Foolish are the generals who ignore the daily intelligence from the trenches.

—Anonymous

KEY CONCEPT

GATHERING THE ISSUES

The first step of the planning process is to *identify the issues.* In preparation for each planning session I conduct for my clients, I meet with the CEO and those senior staff people who will attend the planning session. These meetings are held on a one-on-one basis. This allows each member of the staff, as well as the CEO, the opportunity to open up and offer insights on what's really going on in the company so that the planning session can be more effective. In these meetings, which typically last an hour or more, I hear from each manager about the company's organization, market, customer base, and operations; their roles and responsibilities; and their own vision of the future of the company. Finally, I query them on the issues (or roadblocks) they see in the way of successfully achieving the goals and objectives of the business plan they are about to develop. In other words, I find out where the company is before the planning team puts the plan in place.

KEY CONCEPT

The Interview Process

The standard approach to get people to reveal the real issues facing their organization involves gaining their confidence. Those senior people who are interviewed are assured that all conversations with them will be private. Upon completion of the interviews, an integrated list of issues is developed (with no names attached) to be shared with the participants in the upcoming planning session. In most cases, this process prompts people to be candid.

Over the last 8 years, I have conducted approximately 400 interviews of this nature. Surprisingly, I haven't heard a lot of complaining but, rather, a genuine interest in getting at the issues in order to make the company more successful and a better place to work. I never, in any of my interviews, try to draw out a particular issue. I set the stage and let the persons being interviewed speak their minds. I ask questions to clarify their statements, but I never coach them to pursue a particular issue area.

Gathering and Presenting the Issues

In getting at these issues, my conversation goes something like this: "So you are a $2-million company today and you believe you could be a $10-million company in 5 years. Tell me what changes are necessary to be made in the company in order to achieve this $10-million goal." This question usually opens up the floodgates, uncovering the issues residing in all the elements of the company, including executive management, production and operations (where the revenue is generated), and the staff organizations, including marketing and sales, personnel, finance, and administration.

Each of these interview sessions will often produce anywhere from 5 to 20 issues. Upon completion of these interviews, I integrate the issues (the major issues are often voiced repeatedly by a majority of the persons interviewed) into a set of statements that reflect what I have heard. In maintaining the promised confidentiality, I don't attach names to the issues I have gathered. As mentioned earlier, the first thing I do in the planning session is share with the group the issues they have brought to light. I want to make sure they understand the issues, and if someone questions an issue, I ask for clarification from those who have voiced the issue. Sometimes an issue is discarded if a large majority of the participants don't agree that it's an issue. It's amazing how open and responsive the group becomes—even to such tough issues as "The CEO doesn't delegate" or "There is insufficient accountability by the senior staff."

After I have shared the issues with the group, I put them aside and return to them later in the day when we develop the tactical portion of the plan. This is when we will define annual objectives and near-term actions to address each and every issue.

ISSUES FOR SMALL AND START-UP COMPANIES

Typically, the larger the company, the greater the number and breadth of issues. For small and start-up companies, issues usually arise in the areas of capturing business, acquiring start-up capital and space, hiring employees, and setting up the business in terms of accounting and legal support. Therefore, the array of issues presented in Chapters 4 and 5 may not be highly applicable. On the other hand, it is important to review the issues presented in order to identify those issues you are facing and come up with the necessary actions to eliminate them.

KEY CONCEPT **MAJOR ISSUE CATEGORIES**
Based on my experience in working with more than 70 companies over the last 8 years, I have found that most issues tend to be concentrated among nine major categories, as follows:

1. *Marketing and sales.* Includes new revenue generation.
2. *Personnel and compensation.* Includes hiring and retaining employees.
3. *Communications.* Includes communications up, down, and across the line.
4. *Management and operations.* Includes company organization and revenue production.

5. *Culture.* The heart and soul of the company; culture affects relationships and the working environment.

6. *Systems and processes.* Includes systems, processes, and procedures for operating the company.

7. *Planning.* Includes both long- and short-term planning.

8. *Resources.* Includes staff, equipment, and facilities.

9. *Finance and administration.* Includes finance, accounting, contracts, and office management.

 **INCORPORATING ISSUE-RESOLUTION ACTIONS INTO THE BUSINESS PLAN**

Every company, including yours, has its set of issues that get in the way of growing the company and making it a more successful and enjoyable place to be. It is critical to get at these issues up front, because they are true impediments to successfully implementing the business plan. Raising these issues is akin to picking your head out of the sand, taking a hard look at the monsters in your midst, determining the appropriate responses to eliminate them, and incorporating those response actions into your business plan.

Figure 3.1 illustrates the nine key areas where issues reside. Once the specific issues in each category are identified, approaches for their elimination (issue-resolution strategies and actions) are developed and included in the tactical (near-term) portion of your business plan.

In larger companies, senior management typically raises the issues, but in smaller or start-up companies, the owner raises them. Even if you're the only one raising issues, I strongly suggest getting some feedback on company issues observed by your close associates, accountant, vendors, customers, family, and friends.

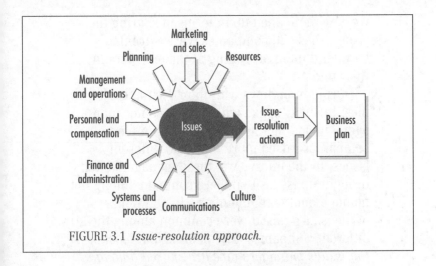

FIGURE 3.1 *Issue-resolution approach.*

 MAJOR ISSUES FACING SMALL TO MEDIUM-SIZED COMPANIES

A description of the relative significance of the issues that most small to medium-sized companies are facing today will be helpful to you later in developing issues facing your company, covered in Chapters 4 and 5. The analysis of the most popular issues is based on a sample of companies I have worked with in the past.

The Sample Companies

For the purposes of this book, I analyzed the issues raised by 20 companies that I have worked with over the past several years. I selected these sample companies based on three criteria: (1) their size, (2) the nature of their service and product offerings, and (3) their degree of responsiveness in describing the issues facing them.

In terms of size, I wanted a representation of both small and medium-sized companies. The 20 companies ranged from less than $1 million in annual revenue to more than $100 million. In terms of what they sold, I wanted a broad representation of products and services. The offerings of the 20 sample companies included computer and telecommunications products and services, real estate management, heavy equipment sales and service, waste recycling, and home remodeling. Although most companies I work with do open up in terms of sharing their issues, these 20 companies were extremely vocal and intent at getting at the monsters in their midst.

During interviews with the 20 sample companies, I usually spoke with 3 to 10 senior managers, including the CEO. The 20 sample companies raised more than 100 different issues. In the interviews, these managers often brought up issues that were common among the management team members. In addition, many of the issues raised were common among the 20 different companies. The point is that *most of the issues managers face are shared among businesses no matter their size or product and service offerings.*

The Major Issues

In order to get at the *major* issues in my analysis, I discarded any issue that was not voiced by at least 5 of the 20 sample companies (25 percent). Based on this criterion, a total of 67 different major issues were raised. Figure 3.2 shows the percentages of these 67 issues, broken down into the 9 issue categories described earlier. As illustrated, the percentages of the 67 major issues, sorted by issue category, ranged from 25 percent (18 major issues) for marketing and sales to 5 percent (4 major issues) for finance and administration. It's clear from Figure 3.2 that marketing and sales (generating new revenues for the company) and personnel and compensation (hiring and retaining employees) are the two categories with the greatest numbers of significant issues, accounting for almost half the major issues cited.

Issue Categories by Number of Responses

Analysis indicated that the 67 major issues were raised 633 times by the 20 sample companies. Recall that for an issue to be considered, at least 5 of the 20 companies had to voice the same issue. Figure 3.3 portrays the distribution of these 633 responses in the 9 issue categories. Again, marketing and sales (158 responses) and

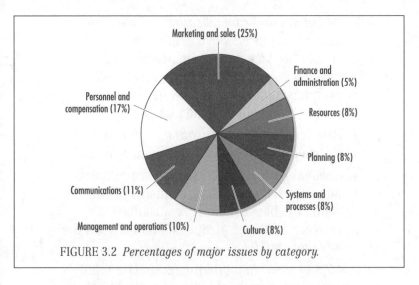

FIGURE 3.2 *Percentages of major issues by category.*

personnel and compensation (106 responses) led the way.

Referring to Figures 3.2 and 3.3, we see that the distribution of issues by category and the frequency of the 633 issue responses resulted in the same ranking of criticality for the 9 issue categories. It is interesting to examine the most pressing issues voiced by the 20 sample companies. There were 8 issues that were brought up by at least 75 percent of the sample companies:

1. *Marketing and sales.* "Our approach to business development is haphazard and uncoordinated; everybody's doing their own thing. There are no standard business-development practices and procedures in place."

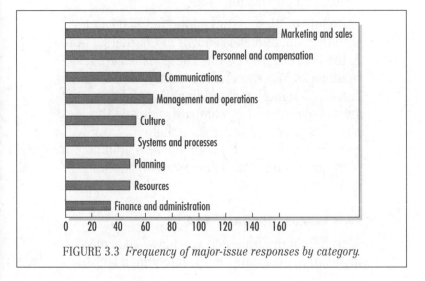

FIGURE 3.3 *Frequency of major-issue responses by category.*

2. *Personnel and compensation.* "We're not rewarding our effective employees sufficiently; we lack management and staff incentives such as a performance-based compensation program and/or a stock-ownership/profit-sharing plan."

3. *Personnel and compensation.* "We don't sufficiently train our management and staff."

4. *Communications.* "There are communication gaps between major elements of our company; between line organizations, between staff organizations, and between the line and staff."

5. *Management and operations.* "Our managers lack accountability and authority; they don't understand their roles, responsibilities, and authorities to carry out their jobs; there's no clear statement of goals and objectives; and we lack position/job descriptions."

6. *Systems and processes.* "We lack standardized, documented, and effective systems, processes, policies, and procedures; we shoot from the hip."

7. *Planning.* "We don't have an agreed-upon common vision, focus, direction, goals, and objectives for the company—a business plan."

8. *Resources.* "We're understaffed; we need to expand our corporate (marketing/sales, human resources, accounting, contracts, financing, administration) and line/technical/operations staff."

Do any of these issues sound familiar? I'm sure they do, and as is shown in Chapters 4 and 5, the list goes on and on. These issues are roadblocks to a successful company and a successful plan implementation and are almost always overlooked by companies during the planning process. Addressing them up front will go a long way toward making your plan (and, more important, your company) considerably more effective.

Two Issues Not Included

A predominant issue that you may feel is missing from the eight just listed might be a lack of sufficient new business in the pipeline. Almost every company I have ever encountered (including my own) could cite this as an issue—even the highly successful companies. There are numerous reasons for the lack of sufficient business, such as the "haphazard and uncoordinated business-development processes" issue mentioned in the list. Others include having an insufficient sales staff, being too busy to market and sell, and not winning competitive bids. A lack of sufficient new business in the pipeline is surely an issue, but it's really the result of a number of other issues, as is discussed in Chapter 4.

It may also be surprising to you that lack of sufficient capital is not shown as a predominant issue. The reason for this may be that many of my clients are established and have overcome the start-up cash-flow issue, although this issue again raises its head for rapidly growing companies—many of my clients are in this exciting position. In addition, most of my clients are service rather than product companies, which often reduces the pressing need to raise money to cover such items as inventory, equipment, and so on. Also, most of my clients have established lines of credit and short-term loans with their banks that often address their issues surrounding the short-term need for capital.

If you need to obtain capital, you should consider developing that classical business plan referred to in Chapter 1. The classical business plan combined with the growth-oriented business plan presented in this book will serve you well when you place them both in the hands of potential investors.

KEY CONCEPT **WHERE ISSUES RESIDE**

Issues are either specific to a particular function within a company, or they reside throughout the company. Here the discussion of the issue categories is broken out into *function-specific issues* (presented in Chapter 4) and *companywide issues* (presented in Chapter 5). The reason for treating them as two separate groups is that the resolution of these issues is dealt with differently depending on where they reside in the organization. Figure 3.4 presents an organization chart for a company. The four functions of marketing and sales, human resources, operations, and finance and administration are performed in every company, no matter what its size. Larger companies have separate departments to perform these four functions, and the respective department head typically handles resolution of the issues. For the smaller company, the owner typically addresses the issues in these four areas. Issues that stem directly from the activities in these four disciplines are what I call *function-specific*.

KEY CONCEPT — Function-Specific Issues

Function-specific issues are predominantly found in four key areas of a company:

1. Marketing and sales
2. Personnel and compensation
3. Management and operations
4. Finance and administration

Marketing and sales issues refer primarily to the marketing and sales organization shown in Figure 3.4, which is responsible for getting the company's product or service into the marketplace. Marketing and sales issues typically stem from a lack of proficiency in keeping the business pipeline sufficiently filled. Several major marketing and sales issues were previously mentioned; they include haphazard and uncoordinated business-development processes, an

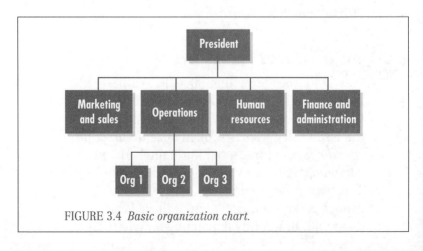

FIGURE 3.4 *Basic organization chart.*

insufficient sales staff, managers being too busy to market and sell, and not winning competitive bids. This is not to say that the operations organization or the president aren't part of the problem, but it is generally up to the marketing and sales organization to be a major factor in resolving the marketing and sales issues.

Personnel and compensation issues refer primarily to the human resources (HR) organization shown in Figure 3.4, which is responsible for the recruiting and retention of employees. Major HR issues are a lack of employee incentives and a lack of an employee training program. These types of issues might stem from any organization in the company, but, as in the case of marketing and sales, it is generally up to HR to take a lead role in resolving the personnel and compensation issues.

Management and operations issues refer primarily to the operations organization shown in Figure 3.4. This is where the revenue is generated in the company, through manufacturing products, providing services, or making wholesale and retail sales, to name a few possibilities. The major management and operations issue is managers lacking accountability and authority. There is no question that the CEO and other staff organizations may have a hand in creating the management and operations issues, but it is usually up to the operations organization(s) to take the lead in resolving them.

Finance and administration issues refer primarily to the finance and administration organization shown in Figure 3.4, which is responsible for all the company's financial tracking and planning as well as the administration (sometimes performed by the HR organization) of the company. Major finance and administration issues are an inadequate financial system and costs being out of control. Again, finance and administration issues may stem from other elements of the company, but it is generally up to this organization to resolve them.

Chapter 4 describes the major issues stemming from these four organization-specific issue categories and presents approaches for dealing with them.

KEY CONCEPT **Companywide Issues**

Companywide issues are generally found throughout the enterprise, and resolving these issues usually requires a companywide effort involving senior managers throughout the company. The key companywide issues can usually be found in the following five areas:

1. Communications
2. Culture
3. Systems and processes
4. Planning
5. Resources

Communications issues are highly prevalent and typically appear throughout the company's infrastructure. The major communications issue is communications gaps up, down, and across the line. The CEO must usually play a major part in resolving these issues, but it is up to all senior managers to become part of the solution.

Culture issues show up throughout an organization, but I believe it is top management (specifically the president or CEO) that sets the culture and that must take the leading steps in modifying it if necessary. The major culture issue is a lack of accountability throughout the company. Virginia O'Brien indicates that "culture is the accumulated shared values, beliefs, attitudes, assumptions, interpretations, habits, customs, practices, knowledge, and behaviors of a group of people which bind them together."[1] She goes on to say that "cultural change messages must come from senior managers. . . ." Therefore, I believe it is primarily up to the CEO, working with other senior managers, to address culture issues.

Systems and processes issues also generally show up in all elements of the organization. The major systems and processes issue is a lack of standardized systems. Systems and processes issues abound—they show up in finance and administration as poor financial reporting, and in operations as ineffective monitoring of the quality of the product or service or a lack of processes for developing and delivering the company's products and services. In HR, systems and processes issues show up as ineffective hiring processes and poor employee performance tracking and compensation systems, in marketing and sales as ineffective tracking of sales and marketing activities, and at the CEO level in poor reporting of all company operations. Again, these issues must be addressed as they present themselves in each of the operational elements of the company.

Planning issues show up across the board, as well. The major planning issue is a lack of a business plan. The CEO must take on the resolution of issues surrounding the company's business plan, but each organization must address particular planning issues internally.

Finally, *resources issues* are typically present in a number of organizations—they focus on staff, facilities, and equipment. The major resource issue is a lack of sufficient staff. Senior management in organizations facing this issue must be part of dealing with it.

Chapter 5 describes the major issues stemming from these five companywide issue categories and presents approaches for dealing with them.

END POINT

The first step of the three-step planning process is to identify the issues that stand in the way of your organization's success. In addition to your own definition of these issues, it is important to speak with your key employees and company advisors to gather their indications of issues that need to be addressed.

Issues facing most small to medium-sized companies fall into nine categories:

1. Marketing and Sales
2. Personnel and compensation
3. Communications
4. Management and operations
5. Culture
6. Systems and processes
7. Planning

8. Resources

9. Finance and administration

Marketing and sales, and personnel and compensation, typically account for the majority of issues facing most companies.

Following the definition of the issues, activities to eliminate them need to be identified for later inclusion into your business plan. The nine categories of issues can be viewed as being either function-specific or companywide, the distinction being where within the company the issues need to be addressed.

With the background of issues presented in this chapter, you are now prepared to undertake the development of your own function-specific issues, as presented in Chapter 4, and companywide issues, as presented in Chapter 5. Gathering the issues that stand in the way of success is the first step toward making a plan that will go a long way toward ensuring your organization's growth and success. Listen to what your employees and others have to say about your issues—whether from a functional or a companywide perspective. Acting to eliminate these issues will make a major difference in your organization's performance. Recalling the opening quote from this chapter, it would be foolish to ignore "the daily intelligence from the trenches."

Function-Specific Issues and Appropriate Response Options

Issues faced by small to medium-sized companies are broken into four function-specific categories (discussed in this chapter) and five companywide categories (discussed in Chapter 5). The four function-specific categories are the following:

1. Marketing and sales
2. Personnel and compensation
3. Management and operations
4. Finance and administration

The major issues in each of the four function-specific categories are identified based on an analysis of 20 companies of varying sizes and product and service offerings. The relative frequency of these function-specific issues is also presented to give you a sense of the prevalence of each issue across the 20 sample companies. These examples of issues facing these 20 companies will provide you with a basis for identifying your own issues as you complete the issue-identification exercises.

APPROACH TO ISSUE RESOLUTION

In addition to examples of issues, suggested issue-resolution approaches are also provided to support you in completing the exercises on how to deal with your own function-specific issues. Although the response options presented here and in Chapter 5 have been effective in other companies, they are not meant to represent the *only* answers to the issues at hand, because I don't have first-hand knowledge of your company, your resources, or your particular issues. I suggest that these responses are generally applicable based on my experience, having worked with more than 70 companies of different sizes, product and service offerings, and markets over the last 8 years. There is no guarantee that these responses will completely deal with your issues because there may be circumstances in your company that make it inappropriate to implement them. They are presented for your consideration and for assistance in developing your plan—use them as you see fit. In reality, you're the most appropriate one to determine the course of action to eliminate your company's issues because you deal with them each and every day.

KEY CONCEPT   Issue-Resolution Timeframe

In most cases, issues should be addressed immediately. If you have limited resources, prioritize your issues and work on the most critical ones first. Near-term actions to address every major issue confronting you should show up in the action plan portion of your business plan (immediate actions to be completed in the next 30 days; see Chapter 8). For those issues that will require some time to address completely, annual objectives (to be accomplished prior to the end of your fiscal year) should be defined for inclusion in your business plan, as well. Therefore, the suggested responses to the issues presented in the tables in this chapter for each of the nine issue categories are meant to lead to your business plan action items and perhaps to your annual objectives, as well.

Consider Using Consultants

In a number of cases, the suggested response strategy involves retaining the services of a consultant to support you in addressing particular issues in each of the nine issue categories. The advantage of using consultants is that they bring a particular expertise to bear on solving a problem and you have no long-term commitment. In other instances, it may make more sense to hire a full-time employee to handle the issue. The decision as to which way to go depends on a number of factors, including affordability and the nature (long- or short-term) of the requirement.

Documenting Your Business Plan

You are about to begin the documentation of your business plan, starting with your issues. Using a blank pad of paper or your computer, you will first document your major issues and approaches for their resolution (by completing the exercises in this chapter and in Chapter 5), using the suggested format shown in Appendix A: Your Major Issues and Approaches for Resolution.

In developing your list of issues and approaches for their resolution, try to keep the number of issues in each category to less than five. Limiting the number enables you to focus on the major issues. If you feel strongly about exceeding the suggested number, by all means do so in compiling your list of issues to be dealt with.

The second document you will create (by completing the exercises in Chapters 6 to 9) is your business plan, using the format shown in Appendix B: Your Business Plan. These two appendixes are referred to for the remainder of the business-plan-development activity.

 **MARKETING AND SALES ISSUES AND RESPONSE OPTIONS**

The marketing and sales category produces the largest number of issues. These issues center on the all-important activity of identifying and capturing new business. Referring to Figure 4.1, 18 major marketing and sales issues were raised by the 20 sample companies. As indicated, these issues ranged in frequency from 80 percent (16 companies raised the issue) to 25 percent (5 companies raised the issue).

The top marketing and sales issue is a haphazard and uncoordinated approach to market-

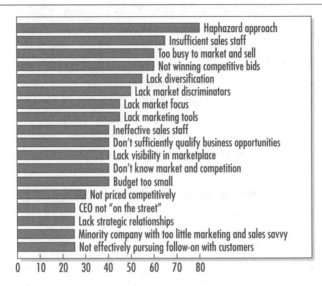

Haphazard approach
Insufficient sales staff
Too busy to market and sell
Not winning competitive bids
Lack diversification
Lack market discriminators
Lack market focus
Lack marketing tools
Ineffective sales staff
Don't sufficiently qualify business opportunities
Lack visibility in marketplace
Don't know market and competition
Budget too small
Not priced competitively
CEO not "on the street"
Lack strategic relationships
Minority company with too little marketing and sales savvy
Not effectively pursuing follow-on with customers

0 10 20 30 40 50 60 70 80

FIGURE 4.1 *Percentages of companies raising major marketing and sales issues.*

ing and sales. At first cut, this definitely appears to be a marketing and sales–category issue. Digging deeper, the real issue here is a lack of effective systems and processes in the marketing and sales operation. Perhaps this issue should fall into the systems and processes category. As you review the issues presented, this issue (and a number of other issues discussed throughout this chapter and Chapter 5) could be placed in more than one of the nine issue categories. Addressing the issue, regardless of which category it falls into, is the important undertaking.

The 18 major marketing and sales issues and the frequency with which these issues were raised are discussed following.

1. *Haphazard approach to business development (80 percent).*   "Our approach to business development is haphazard and uncoordinated; everybody's doing their own thing. There are no standard business-development practices and procedures in place."

2. *Insufficient sales staff (65 percent).*   "We lack sufficient business-development (sales) staff."

3. *Too busy to market and sell (60 percent).* "We're too focused on doing the work

instead of building our business; we don't have the time and/or inclination to develop business, and too few key people are generating business."

4. *Not winning competitive bids (60 percent).* "We are not winning our share of competitive proposals; we lack proposal-preparation skills, resources, systems, and methodologies."

5. *Lack diversification (55 percent).* "We're not reaching all our market; we lack diversification of our client base (all our eggs in too few baskets), our geographical presence, and our product and service offerings."

6. *Lack market discriminators (50 percent).* "We don't have any market discriminators or niches; we're plain old vanilla."

7. *Lack market focus (45 percent).* "We don't know what business we're in—we're all over the place; we don't focus our business pursuit in our core competencies."

8. *Lack marketing tools (45 percent).* "We need marketing tools (e.g., brochures and presentations) or we need to improve our current tools."

9. *Ineffective sales staff (40 percent).* "Our sales staff doesn't possess the proper experience, expertise, contacts, or networks to be effective; we lack business-development leadership."

10. *Don't sufficiently qualify business opportunities (40 percent).* "We don't sufficiently qualify our business opportunities; we do a poor job of gathering market intelligence, our business pursuit is too shotgun, and we're bidding on things we shouldn't be."

11. *Lack visibility in the marketplace (40 percent).* "We are not known in our marketplace; we have no visibility, no image."

12. *Don't know market and competition (40 percent).* "We don't know how to grow our business; we don't know our market sufficiently to identify new business, and we don't understand our competition."

13. *Budget too small (40 percent).* "Our business-development budget doesn't exist or is not sufficient to pursue the level of business we need to grow and prosper; we're not sufficiently investing in our future."

14. *Not priced competitively (30 percent).* "We're losing business because we aren't priced competitively."

15. *CEO not "on the street" (25 percent).* "Our best salespeople (CEO and other senior managers) are not on the street expanding our business." Note that this issue sounds similar to the "too busy" issue cited as issue 3.

16. *Lack strategic relationships (25 percent).* "We lack strategic relationships with other companies that would increase our exposure in the marketplace."

17. *Minority company with too little marketing and sales savvy (25 percent).* "We are (or have been) in the minority set-aside program, and now that we are about to graduate (or have graduated), we don't know how to proceed to acquire business competitively."

18. *Not effectively pursuing follow-on with customers (25 percent).* "We're not pursuing follow-on business effectively with our current clients."

After defining your marketing and sales issues in Exercise 1, identify actions to eliminate the issues in Exercise 2. Table 4.1 presents suggestions for dealing with these marketing and sales issues.

EXERCISE 1: DEFINE YOUR MARKETING AND SALES ISSUES

Review the list of 18 marketing and sales issues presented in the preceding text and consider any others that are not mentioned. Write your marketing and sales issues in your Major Issues and Approaches for Resolution document (see Appendix A).

EXERCISE 2: DEFINE YOUR RESPONSE TO MARKETING AND SALES ISSUES

For each marketing and sales issue you have identified in Exercise 1, develop a response using the examples presented in Table 4.1 or, as an alternative, define your own responses. Write these issue responses in your Major Issues and Approaches for Resolution document (see Appendix A).

TABLE 4.1 RESPONSE OPTIONS FOR MARKETING AND SALES ISSUES

Issue 1. Our approach to business development is haphazard and un-coordinated; everybody's doing their own thing. There are no standard business-development practices and procedures in place.

- Use your business plan to clearly define senior manager business-development objectives—monitor their progress and hold them accountable.
- Hold regularly scheduled business-development meetings to coordinate and monitor all business-development actions.
- Develop a standard (companywide) set of business-development processes and procedures.

Issue 2. We lack sufficient business-development (sales) staff.

- If affordable, hire additional salespeople. If not, consider reducing costs in other areas to make funds available.
- Hire part-time sales people or consultants. Attempt to pay them on a commission basis.

Issue 3. We're too focused on doing the work instead of building our business; we don't have the time and/or inclination to develop business, and too few people are generating business.

- Use your business plan to clearly define senior manager business-development objectives—monitor their progress and hold them accountable.
- If affordable, hire additional marketers or salespeople.
- Retain sales consultants or contractors.

Issue 4. We are not winning our share of competitive proposals; we lack proposal preparation skills, resources, systems, and methodologies.

- Review your business-development processes (identification, qualification, pursuit, and capture)—identify and address faults hindering your proposal preparation success.
- Speak to the decision makers re why your proposal was unsuccessful and correct deficiencies in the future.
- If affordable, hire personnel or retain consultants with proposal-writing skills.

TABLE 4.1 *(Continued)*

● Train your proposal writers.

Issue 5. We're not reaching all our market; we lack diversification of our client base (all our eggs in too few baskets), our geographical presence, and our product and service offerings.

● Use your business plan to clearly define new business-diversification goals and objectives.

● Hire or retain the services of a business developer who can get you entrée into new markets.

● Consider acquisitions.

Issue 6. We don't have any market discriminators or niches; we're plain old vanilla.

● Develop strategies and supporting tactics to provide you with future discriminators (see Chapters 7 and 8).

● Consider acquisitions.

Issue 7. We don't know what business we're in—we're all over the place; we don't focus our business pursuit in our core competencies.

● Define the products and services you will sell and the clients you will pursue (see Chapter 7, Mission Statement Question 1). When pursuing new business, ask yourself, "Is this opportunity in support of my business plan?"

Issue 8. We need marketing tools (e.g., brochures, capability statements, etc.) or we need to improve our current tools.

● Develop a budget and plan for upgrading your marketing collateral.

● Retain a marketing consultant.

Issue 9. Our sales staff doesn't possess the proper experience, expertise, contacts, or networks to be effective; we lack business-development leadership.

● Spend more time with your sales staff—develop sales objectives with them and manage their progress.

● Spend time with them in front of customers.

● Train or replace your sales staff.

Issue 10. We don't sufficiently qualify our business opportunities; we do a poor job of gathering market intelligence, our business pursuit is too shotgun, and we're bidding on things we shouldn't be.

● Develop a prospect questionnaire to be used when pursuing new business.

● Hold regularly scheduled business-development meetings to coordinate all business-development actions.

● Develop and use a bid/no-bid decision-making tool.

● Develop a standard (companywide) business-development process and supporting procedures.

TABLE 4.1 (Continued)

- Retain a business-development expert to support the development of a process.

Issue 11. We are not known in our marketplace; we have no visibility, no image.

- Develop a marketing plan addressing advertising and public relations and a budget to support it.
- Develop market visibility goals and objectives (see Chapters 7 and 8 for examples).

Issue 12. We don't know how to grow our business; we don't know our market sufficiently to identify new business, and we don't understand our competition.

- Develop and implement your business plan.
- Hire, on a full-time, part-time, or consultant basis, someone with a marketing and sales track record in your market.

Issue 13. Our business-development budget doesn't exist or is not sufficient to pursue the level of business we need to grow and prosper; we're not sufficiently investing in our future.

- Find the money—you won't succeed without marketing and sales.
- Consider investing profit into the business-development activity or selling an interest in the company to raise capital.
- Borrow the money.

Issue 14. We're losing business because we aren't priced competitively.

- Determine your competition's rates.
- Review your costs with an aim toward identifying opportunities to reduce them.
- Develop budgets and manage them through monthly reviews.
- Hire an expert to provide counsel.

Issue 15. Our best salespeople (CEO and other senior managers) are not "on the street" expanding our business.

- CEO and senior managers champion new business objectives.

Issue 16. We lack strategic relationships with other companies that would increase our exposure in the marketplace.

- Develop market visibility goals and objectives (see Chapters 7 and 8 for examples).
- Set up meetings with company executives you would like to team with—present your capabilities.
- Get involved in business or professional organizations; meet people and network.

Issue 17. We are (or have been) in the minority set-aside program and now that we are about to graduate or have graduated, we don't know how to proceed to acquire business competitively.

TABLE 4.1 (Continued)

- Develop and implement your business plan.
- Hire or obtain the services of an expert business developer familiar with your market.

Issue 18. We're not pursuing follow-on business effectively with our current clients.

- In your business plan, assign business follow-on objectives to senior managers.
- Develop a client questionnaire addressing your company's performance and include a marketing element—get in front of your clients (face to face).
- Train those responsible or hire someone who will close follow-on business.

PERSONNEL AND COMPENSATION ISSUES AND RESPONSE OPTIONS

Personnel and compensation is the second most popular area where obstacles to growth and success are raised. These issues center on the hiring and retention of employees. Figure 4.2 shows 11 major personnel and compensation issues raised by the twenty sample companies. These issues ranged in frequency from 80 percent (16 companies raised the issue) to 30 percent (6 companies raised the issue); lack of employee incentives and lack of employee training programs led the lot. A brief statement of these 11 issues follows:

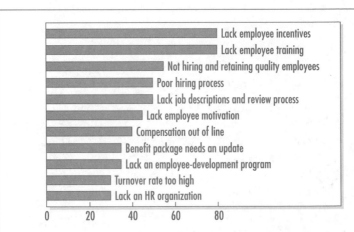

FIGURE 4.2 *Percentages of companies raising major personnel and compensation issues.*

1. *Lack employee incentives (80 percent).* "We're not rewarding our effective employees sufficiently; we lack management and staff incentives, such as a performance-based compensation program and/or a stock-ownership/profit-sharing plan."

2. *Lack employee training (80 percent).* "We don't sufficiently train our management and staff."

3. *Not hiring and retaining quality employees (55 percent).* "We need to do a better job of hiring and retaining quality employees."

4. *Poor hiring process (50 percent).* "We're not able to hire the skilled people we need and/or we take too long in filling our staff openings; our hiring process is not effective."

5. *Lack job descriptions and an employee review process (50 percent).* "We lack job descriptions and a regularly scheduled employee performance evaluation and salary review process."

6. *Lack employee motivation (45 percent).* "There's a general lack of employee motivation and morale, especially in our field operations."

7. *Compensation out of line (40 percent).* "Our salary structure, sales commissions, and bonus program are out of line with the competition, affecting rates (they're too high) or our ability to hire and retain good people (they're too low)."

8. *Benefits package needs an update (35 percent).* "Our benefits package needs to be updated and expanded."

9. *Lack an employee-development program (35 percent).* "We lack an employee-development program; our employees feel dead-ended with no clear career path." Note that this issue sounds similar to the "lack of training" issue cited as issue 2.

10. *Turnover rate too high (30 percent).* "Our turnover rate is too high."

11. *Lack an HR organization (30 percent).* "We lack an HR organization or need to expand the HR staff."

After defining your personnel and compensation issues in Exercise 3, identify actions to eliminate these issues in Exercise 4. Table 4.2 presents suggestions for dealing with these 11 personnel and compensation issues.

EXERCISE 3: DEFINE YOUR PERSONNEL AND COMPENSATION ISSUES

Review the list of 11 personnel and compensation issues presented in the preceding text and consider any others that are not mentioned. Document your personnel and compensation issues in your Major Issues and Approaches for Resolution document (see Appendix A).

EXERCISE 4: DEFINE YOUR RESPONSE TO PERSONNEL AND COMPENSATION ISSUES

For each personnel and compensation issue you have identified in Exercise 3, develop a response using the examples presented in Table 4.2 or, as an alternative, define your own responses. Write these issue responses in your Major Issues and Approaches for Resolution document (see Appendix A).

TABLE 4.2 RESPONSE OPTIONS FOR PERSONNEL AND COMPENSATION ISSUES

Issue 1. We're not rewarding our effective employees sufficiently; we lack management and staff incentives, such as a performance-based compensation program and/or a stock ownership/profit-sharing plan.
- Develop and implement an employee incentive program.
- Retain a compensation or HR consultant.

Issue 2. We don't sufficiently train our management and staff.
- Implement an employee-training program.
- Consider both in-house (senior staff does training) as well as paid seminars.
- Bring trainers in-house.

Issue 3. We need to do a better job of hiring and retaining quality employees.
- Review your benefits and compensation programs.
- Get training in interviewing for key players.

TABLE 4.2 (Continued)

Issue 4. We're not able to hire the skilled people we need and/or we take too long in filling our staff openings; our hiring process is not effective.

- Review your hiring process—make necessary changes.
- Retain the services of a recruiter.
- Implement a recruiting bonus for your current employees.

Issue 5. We lack job descriptions and a regularly scheduled employee performance evaluation and salary review process.

- Prepare job descriptions for every employee.
- Develop and implement an employee performance evaluation and salary review process.
- Retain the services of an HR expert.

Issue 6. There's a general lack of employee motivation and morale, especially in our field operations.

- Increase senior management contact and communications with employees.
- Brief your business plan to all employees.
- Create an employee incentive program.
- Create a company newsletter.
- Look for opportunities to reward employees and broadcast the rewards to all employees.
- Hold regularly scheduled all-hands meetings throughout the company.
- Survey the staff and determine the issues.
- Retain the services of an HR expert.

Issue 7. Our salary structure, sales commissions, and bonus program are out of line with the competition, affecting rates (they're too high) or our ability to hire and retain good people (they're too low).

- Gain an accurate understanding of your competition's compensation program—check available surveys.
- Develop a compensation program in line with your competition.
- Retain the services of an HR expert.

Issue 8. Our benefits package needs to be updated and expanded.

- Gain an accurate understanding of your competition's benefits program—check available surveys.
- Develop a benefits program in line with your competition.
- Retain the services of an HR expert.

Issue 9. We lack an employee-development program; our employees feel dead-ended with no clear career path.

- Conduct an employee survey to determine requirements.
- Implement an employee-development program.
- Retain the services of an HR expert.

> ### TABLE 4.2 (Continued)
>
> *Issue 10.* Our turnover rate is too high.
> - Attempt to gain an understanding as to why employees leave—use exit interviews, and talk to the troops.
> - Review your benefits and compensation program.
> - Retain the services of an HR expert.
>
> *Issue 11.* We lack an HR organization or need to expand the HR staff.
> - If affordable, expand your HR organization.
> - If not affordable, consider bringing on part-time or consultant HR support.

 MANAGEMENT AND OPERATIONS
CONCEPT **ISSUES AND RESPONSE OPTIONS**

The issues surrounding management and operations deal with how the company is managed. As shown in Figure 4.3, 7 management and operations issues were raised by the 20 sample companies. These ranged in frequency from 90 percent (18 companies raised the issue) to 25 percent (5 companies raised the issue); the issue of managers lacking accountability and authority led the lot. A brief statement of these seven issues follows:

1. *Managers lack accountability and authority (90 percent).* "Our managers don't understand their roles, responsibilities, and authorities to carry out their jobs; there's no

FIGURE 4.3 *Percentages of companies raising major management and operations issues.*

clear statement of goals and objectives, and we lack position descriptions."

2. *Lack sufficient infrastructure (55 percent).* "We need to make an investment in our infrastructure (e.g., marketing and sales, human resources, finance and accounting, and quality assurance)."

3. *Lack structured management organization (55 percent).* "We lack a structured management organization, authorities, reporting mechanisms; no clear picture of the organization and lines of authority; who's in charge?"

4. *Not sufficiently servicing customers (35 percent).* "We're not servicing our customers as effectively as we need to; management doesn't relate to our customers."

5. *Insufficient quality assurance (35 percent).* "Too many things are falling through the cracks; we're growing too fast and we need a formalized quality-assurance program."

6. *Insufficient project and account management (30 percent).* "We lack sufficient project and account management and reporting systems; we need regularly scheduled project or account reviews."

7. *Management team lacks leadership (25 percent).* "Our management team (senior and middle management) lacks leadership."

After defining your management and operations issues in Exercise 5, define approaches to eliminate these issues in Exercise 6. Table 4.3 presents suggestions for dealing with these seven management and operations issues.

EXERCISE 5: DEFINE YOUR MANAGEMENT AND OPERATIONS ISSUES

Review the list of seven management and operations issues presented in the preceding text and consider any others that are not mentioned. Document your management and operations issues in your Major Issues and Approaches for Resolution document (see Appendix A).

EXERCISE 6: DEFINE YOUR RESPONSE TO MANAGEMENT AND OPERATIONS ISSUES

For each management and operations issue you have identified in Exercise 5, develop a response using the examples presented in Table 4.3 or, as an alternative, define your own responses. Write these issue responses in your Major Issues and Approaches for Resolution document (see Appendix A).

TABLE 4.3 RESPONSE OPTIONS FOR MANAGEMENT AND OPERATIONS ISSUES

Issue 1. Our managers don't understand their roles, responsibilities, and authorities to carry out their jobs; there's no clear statement of goals and objectives, and we lack position descriptions.

- Prepare management position descriptions describing roles, responsibilities, and authorities—include objectives defined in your business plan.
- Create a companywide authority matrix clearly defining authorities of all levels of management.

Issue 2. We need to make an investment in our infrastructure (e.g., marketing and sales, HR, finance and accounting, and quality assurance).

- Develop a budget for these overhead positions, prioritize, and hire as affordable.
- Consider part-time employees or consultants initially.

Issue 3. We lack a structured management organization, authorities, reporting mechanisms; no clear picture of the organization and lines of authority; who's in charge?

- Prepare management position descriptions describing roles, responsibilities, and authorities—include objectives defined in your business plan.
- Develop and distribute an organization chart.

Issue 4. We're not servicing our customers as effectively as we need to; management doesn't relate to our customers.

- Develop a client questionnaire addressing your company's performance and get senior management in front of clients (face to face) to better understand the issues.
- Get training in customer relations for management.
- Get management in touch with reality or get new managers.

Issue 5. Too many things are falling through the cracks; we're growing too fast and we need a formalized quality-assurance program.

- Poll your management team for suggestions regarding a quality-assurance program.
- Put a quality-assurance program in place.

> ### TABLE 4.3   (Continued)
>
> ● Retain the services of a quality-assurance expert to assist in charting your course.
>
> *Issue 6.*   We lack sufficient project and account management and reporting systems; we need regularly scheduled project and account reviews.
>
> ● Develop a project and account review process and hold regularly scheduled performance reviews.
>
> *Issue 7.*   Our management team (senior and middle management) lacks leadership.
>
> ● Get leadership training for management.
>
> ● Hire new management.

 FINANCE AND ADMINISTRATION
CONCEPT   **ISSUES AND RESPONSE OPTIONS**

The issues in finance and administration deal with financial reporting and operations. As shown in Figure 4.4, four major finance and administration issues were raised by the sample companies. These issues ranged in frequency from 60 percent (12 companies raised the issue) to 30 percent (6 companies raised the issue). The leading finance/administration issue "inadequate financial system" led the list. A brief statement of these four finance and administration issues follows:

1. *Inadequate financial system (60 percent).* "Our financial management and reporting

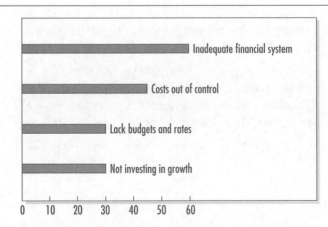

FIGURE 4.4 *Percentages of companies raising major finance and administration issues.*

system requires upgrading; this is hurting our financial position and not effectively providing our corporate management and operating organizations with timely and accurate financial information."

2. *Costs out of control (45 percent).* "Our overhead is too high; we need to take better control of our costs."

3. *Lack budgets and rates (30 percent).* "We need to develop budgets and rates and a system to track them."

4. *Not investing in our growth (30 percent).* "We're not investing in our growth; we need to make an investment (perhaps raise capital) for space, equipment, automation, facilities, staff, technology, marketing, and so on."

After defining your finance and administration issues in Exercise 7, define approaches to eliminate these issues in Exercise 8. Table 4.4 presents suggestions for dealing with these four finance and administration issues.

EXERCISE 7: DEFINE YOUR FINANCE AND ADMINISTRATION ISSUES

Review the list of four finance and administration issues presented in the preceding text and consider any others that are not mentioned. Document your finance and administration issues in your Major Issues and Approaches for Resolution document (see Appendix A).

EXERCISE 8: DEFINE YOUR RESPONSE TO FINANCE AND ADMINISTRATION ISSUES

For each finance and administration issue you have identified in Exercise 7, develop a response using the examples presented in Table 4.4 or, as an alternative, define your own responses. Write these issue responses in your Major Issues and Approaches for Resolution document (see Appendix A).

TABLE 4.4 RESPONSE OPTIONS FOR FINANCE AND ADMINISTRATION ISSUES

Issue 1.   Our financial management and reporting system requires upgrading; this is hurting our financial position and not effectively providing our corporate management and operating organizations with timely and accurate financial information.

- Poll the management team to develop financial reporting requirements.
- Develop and implement an upgraded financial reporting system.
- Retain the services of an expert to develop the system.

Issue 2.   Our overhead is too high; we need to take better control of our costs.

- Review current costs and identify areas where cost cutting is feasible.
- Develop a budget and manage it.
- Retain an expert to make recommendations.

Issue 3.   We need to develop budgets and rates and a system to track them.

- Develop a budget and manage it through regularly scheduled reviews.
- Retain an expert to support the development of the budget.

Issue 4.   We're not investing in our growth; we need to make an investment (perhaps raise capital) for space, equipment, automation, facilities, staff, technology, marketing, and so on.

- Review needs and develop a budget to address them.
- Consider securing a loan or other means of raising capital to meet these needs.

END POINT

This chapter has identified issues and developed responses for *function-specific* issues. Chapter 5 focuses on *companywide* issues and response options.

Companywide Issues and Appropriate Response Options

After defining your function-specific issues and responses in the previous chapter, this chapter supports the definition and resolution of your companywide issues. The five companywide issue categories are the following:

1. Communications

2. Culture

3. Systems and processes

4. Planning

5. Resources

The major issues in each of the five companywide categories are identified based on an analysis of the 20 sample companies. Again, examples of issues facing the 20 sample companies, along with suggested issue-resolution approaches, are presented to support you in identifying and dealing with your own companywide issues by completing the exercises. The relative frequency of these companywide issues is also presented to give you a sense of the prevalence of each issue across the 20 sample companies.

COMMUNICATIONS ISSUES AND RESPONSE OPTIONS

The communications issue category has the largest number of issues in the companywide arena. As shown in Figure 5.1, 7 major communications issues were raised by the 20 sample companies. These issues ranged in frequency from 80 percent (16 companies raised the issue) to 35 percent (7 companies raised the issue); the hottest issue was communications gaps between major elements of the company. A brief statement of these seven issues follows:

1. *Communications gaps (80 percent).* "There are communication gaps between major elements of our company—between line organizations, between staff organizations, and between the line and staff."

2. *Employees not getting the word (60 percent).* "Employees (and middle management) are not getting the word from the top and this affects morale; a sense that senior management doesn't care."

3. *Poor field employee relationships (55 percent).* "We don't have a good relationship with the management and staff in our field offices."

4. *CEO doesn't communicate (50 percent).* "The CEO doesn't communicate effectively with the senior staff; there is no clear under-

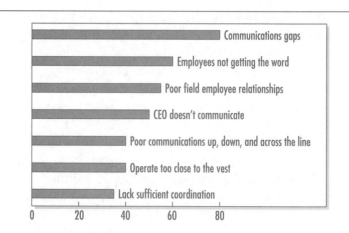

FIGURE 5.1 *Percentages of companies raising major communications issues.*

standing of expectations because we can't get to the CEO."

5. *Poor communications up, down, and across the line (40 percent).* "We don't communicate; we lack communications up, down, and across the line." Note that this issue sounds like the communications gap described in issue 1.

6. *Operate too close to the vest (40 percent).* "The financial well-being and future plans of the company are held too close to the vest; we don't know how the company is doing and where it's going."

7. *Lack sufficient coordination (35 percent).* "We don't coordinate very well; we don't have sufficient meetings and/or meetings are not run efficiently; no agendas are published and meetings are not regularly scheduled."

After defining your communications issues in Exercise 9, define approaches to eliminate these issues in Exercise 10. Table 5.1 presents suggested approaches for dealing with these seven communications issues.

EXERCISE 9: DEFINE YOUR COMMUNICATIONS ISSUES

Review the list of seven communications issues presented in the preceding text and consider any others that are not mentioned. Document your communications issues in your Major Issues and Approaches for Resolution document (see Appendix A).

EXERCISE 10: DEFINE YOUR RESPONSE TO COMMUNICATIONS ISSUES

For each communications issue you have identified in Exercise 9, develop a response using the examples presented in Table 5.1 or, as an alternative, define your own responses. Write these issue responses in your Major Issues and Approaches for Resolution document (see Appendix A).

TABLE 5.1 RESPONSE OPTIONS FOR COMMUNICATIONS ISSUES

Issue 1. There are communications gaps between major elements of our company—between line organizations, between staff organizations, and between the line and staff.

- Hold regularly scheduled senior staff meetings.
- Hold monthly review of annual objectives meeting (see Chapter 9) with senior staff.
- Hold regularly scheduled (e.g., quarterly) cross-briefings between operational elements of the company.
- Increase senior management contact and communications with employees.
- Brief your business plan to all employees.
- Create a company newsletter.
- Hold regular (quarterly) all-hands meetings throughout the company.
- Survey the staff and determine the issues.
- Retain the services of a communications expert.

Issue 2. Employees (and middle management) are not getting the word from the top and this affects morale; a sense that senior management doesn't care.

- Increase senior management contact and communications with employees.
- Brief your business plan to all employees.
- Create a company newsletter.
- Hold regular (quarterly) all-hands meetings throughout the company.
- Survey the staff and determine the issues.
- Retain the services of a communications expert.

Issue 3. We don't have a good relationship with our management and staff in our field offices.

- Have corporate executives visit the field on a regular basis—brief regarding what's going on with the rest of the company.
- Have CEO brief your business plan to the field offices.
- Create a company newsletter.
- Hold regular (quarterly) all-hands meetings throughout the company.
- Survey the staff and determine the issues.
- Retain the services of a communications expert.

Issue 4. The CEO doesn't communicate effectively with the senior staff; there is no clear understanding of expectations because we can't get to the CEO.

TABLE 5.1 (Continued)

- Hold regularly scheduled senior staff meetings.
- Survey the senior staff and determine the issues.
- Retain the services of a communications expert.
- Have CEO find opportunities to work closer with your senior staff.
- Have CEO and senior staff attend a leadership and communications training program.
- In your business plan, clearly define senior manager objectives—monitor and discuss their progress, and hold them accountable.

Issue 5.   We don't communicate; we lack communications up, down, and across the line.

- Hold regularly scheduled senior staff meetings.
- Hold monthly review of annual objectives meeting (see Chapter 9) with senior staff.
- Increase senior management contact and communications with employees.
- Brief your business plan to all employees.
- Create a company newsletter.
- Hold regular (quarterly) all-hands meetings throughout the company.
- Survey the staff and determine the issues.
- Retain the services of a communications expert.

Issue 6.   The financial well being and future plans of the company are held too close to the vest; we don't know how the company is doing and where it's going.

- Develop and implement your business plan.
- As part of the business planning process, have CEO share financials with senior staff.
- Brief the plan to the entire company.

Issue 7.   We don't coordinate very well; we don't have sufficient meetings and/or meetings are not run efficiently; no agendas are published and meetings are not regularly scheduled.

- Hold regularly scheduled senior staff meetings (see Chapter 10).
- Hold monthly review of annual objectives meeting (see Chapter 9) with senior staff.
- Create an agenda and distribute prior to each meeting—stick to it.
- At beginning of meeting, have chair announce meeting objective and duration—stick to it.
- Get training in running meetings.
- Retain the services of a communications expert.

 **CULTURE ISSUES AND RESPONSE OPTIONS**

Culture issues are perhaps the most difficult to deal with because they involve personalities, interrelationships, and management style. As shown in Figure 5.2, 5 major culture issues were raised by the 20 sample companies. These issues ranged in frequency from 65 percent (13 companies raised the issue) to 35 percent (7 companies raised the issue); lack of accountability was the culture issue cited most often. A brief statement of these five issues follows:

1. *Lack accountability (65 percent).* "We lack accountability, credibility, and consistency at all levels; there's no sense of urgency in meeting commitments." Note that this issue is similar to management and operations issue 1, lack of management accountability and authority, cited in Chapter 4.

2. *Don't empower staff (60 percent).* "We don't empower our staff, give them roles, responsibility, and authority and allow them the opportunity to make mistakes; we don't let managers manage."

3. *CEO doesn't delegate (55 percent).* "The CEO (and/or senior management) doesn't delegate; he or she micromanages and is too tied up in the nitty-gritty to do what he or she does best—growing the company."

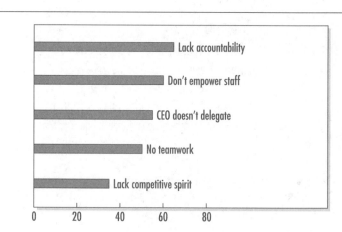

FIGURE 5.2 *Percentages of companies raising major culture issues.*

4. *No teamwork (50 percent).* "We don't function as a team; senior managers care only
about their own organizations and don't take
a company perspective."

5. *Lack competitive spirit (35 percent).* "We
need a more entrepreneurial and competitive
culture in the company."

After defining your culture issues in Exercise
11, define approaches to eliminate these issues
in Exercise 12. Table 5.2 presents response
options for dealing with these five culture
issues.

**EXERCISE 11: DEFINE YOUR CULTURE
ISSUES**

Review the list of seven culture issues presented in the preceding text
and consider any others that are not mentioned. Document your culture issues in your Major Issues and Approaches for Resolution document (see Appendix A).

**EXERCISE 12: DEFINE YOUR RESPONSE
TO CULTURE ISSUES**

For each culture issue you have identified in Exercise 11, develop a
response using the examples presented in Table 5.2 or, as an alternative, define your own responses. Write these issue responses in
your Major Issues and Approaches for Resolution document (see
Appendix A).

 **SYSTEMS AND PROCESSES ISSUES
AND RESPONSE OPTIONS**

Systems and processes are a critical issue category because they often permeate every element
of a company. As shown in Figure 5.3, 6 major
systems and processes issues were raised by the
20 sample companies. These issues ranged in
frequency from 75 percent (15 companies raised
the issue) to 25 percent (5 companies raised the

TABLE 5.2 RESPONSE OPTIONS FOR CULTURE ISSUES

Issue 1. We lack accountability, credibility, and consistency at all levels; there's no sense of urgency in meeting commitments.

- Accountability will come about through the implementation of your business plan (see Part 4).
- Get leadership training for the CEO and other senior managers.

Issue 2. We don't empower our staff, give them roles, responsibility, and authority and allow them the opportunity to make mistakes; we don't let managers manage.

- Prepare management position descriptions describing roles, responsibilities, and authorities.
- Get leadership training for the CEO and other senior managers.

Issue 3. The CEO (and/or senior management) doesn't delegate; he or she micromanages and is too tied up in the nitty-gritty to do what he or she does best—growing the company.

- Get leadership training for the CEO and other senior managers.

Issue 4. We don't function as a team; senior managers care only about their own organizations and don't take a company perspective.

- Get leadership training for the CEO and other senior managers.
- Hold regularly scheduled senior staff meetings—look for opportunities to support a team effort.

Issue 5. We need a more entrepreneurial and competitive culture in the company.

- Implement a sales incentive program for all employees throughout the company.
- Communicate the need for all employees to play a role in effecting sales.
- Provide sales training to selected staff.

issue); the issue of lacking standardized systems led the lot. A brief statement of these six issues follows:

1. *Lack standardized systems (75 percent).* "We lack standardized, documented, and effective systems, processes, policies, and procedures; we shoot from the hip."
2. *Lack policies and procedures (55 percent).* "It's too loose around here; we need to develop (or expand) a policy and procedure manual and an employee handbook."

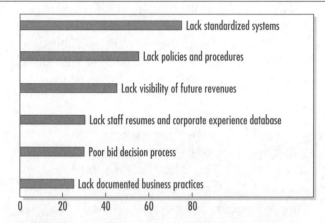

FIGURE 5.3 *Percentages of companies raising major systems and processes issues.*

3. *Lack visibility of future revenues (45 percent).* "We have too short a view of our future revenue stream; we need a system to better track our current business backlog, opportunities, and future revenues."

4. *Lack staff resumes and a corporate experience database (30 percent).* "We need a companywide skills inventory (resumes) and corporate experience database for marketing and bidding purposes."

5. *Poor bid decision process (30 percent).* "We need a more effective process to determine which business opportunities to pursue and bid—a bid/no-bid tool."

6. *Lack documented business practices (25 percent).* "We need to develop, document, and promulgate a set of formal business practices—an operations manual, a project manager's manual, and so on."

EXERCISE 13: DEFINE YOUR SYSTEMS AND PROCESSES ISSUES

Review the list of six systems and processes issues presented in the preceding text and consider any others that are not mentioned. Document your systems and processes issues in your Major Issues and Approaches for Resolution document (see Appendix A).

After defining your systems and processes issues in Exercise 13, define approaches to eliminate these issues in Exercise 14. Table 5.3 presents response options for dealing with these six systems and processes issues.

EXERCISE 14: DEFINE YOUR RESPONSE TO SYSTEMS AND PROCESSES ISSUES

For each systems and processes issue you have identified in Exercise 13, develop a response using the examples presented in Table 5.3 or, as an alternative, define your own responses. Write these issue responses in your Major Issues and Approaches for Resolution document (see Appendix A).

 **PLANNING ISSUES AND RESPONSE OPTIONS**

Planning issues center on a lack of planning and plan implementation. As shown in Figure 5.4, 5 major planning issues were raised by the 20 sample companies. These issues ranged in frequency from 80 percent (16 companies raised the issue) to 30 percent (6 companies raised the issue); the issue of not having a business plan led the lot. A brief statement of these five issues follows:

1. *Don't have a business plan (80 percent).* "We don't have an agreed-upon common vision, focus, direction, goals, and objectives for the company—a business plan."

2. *Lack a marketing and sales plan (50 percent).* "We need a marketing and sales plan to target our markets, determine our entry strategies, and define our future products and services."

3. *Totally reactive management (45 percent).* "We're totally reactive; we don't plan strategically, tactically, or in any other way; we run by the seat of our pants."

4. *Don't implement plans (35 percent).* "We don't implement the plans we do develop; we don't develop action plans as follow-on to our

TABLE 5.3 RESPONSE OPTIONS FOR SYSTEMS AND PROCESSES ISSUES

Issue 1. We lack standardized, documented, and effective systems, processes, policies, and procedures; we shoot from the hip.

- Conduct a survey to determine which systems, processes, policies, and procedures need to be standardized and documented.
- Develop and document standardized systems, processes, policies, and procedures.
- Retain a management consultant to support you in this activity.

Issue 2. It's too loose around here; we need to develop (or expand) a policy and procedure manual and an employee handbook.

- Determine which policy and procedures items need to be developed.
- Develop and document a policy and procedures manual and an employee handbook.
- Retain an HR consultant to support you in this activity.

Issue 3. We have too short a view of our future revenue stream; we need a system to better track our current business backlog, opportunities, and future revenues.

- Develop a business pipeline tracking system (revenue-projection system—see Chapter 8).
- Retain a management consultant to support you in this activity.

Issue 4. We need a companywide skills inventory (resumes) and corporate experience database for marketing and bidding purposes.

- Develop a set of standardized resumes and brief project descriptions for use in proposals.
- If appropriate, develop resume and corporate experience databases for easy access.

Issue 5. We need a more effective process to determine which business opportunities to pursue and bid—a bid/no-bid tool.

- Develop a bid/no-bid decision-making tool—use it regularly.
- Retain an expert to support the tool development.

Issue 6. We need to develop, document, and promulgate a set of formal business practices—an operations manual, a project manager's manual, and so on.

- Determine which business practice items need to be developed.
- Develop and document these business practices.
- Retain a management consultant to support you in this activity.

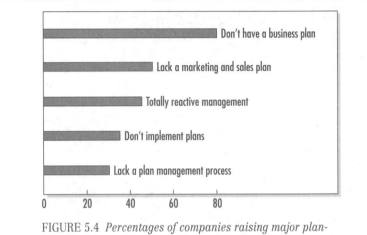

FIGURE 5.4 *Percentages of companies raising major planning issues.*

strategies; we lack the resources, accountability, and commitment (buy-in) to implement our plans."

5. *Lack a plan management process (30 percent).* "We need a process to support the management and implementation of our plans."

After defining your planning issues in Exercise 15, define approaches to eliminate these issues in Exercise 16. Table 5.4 presents response options for dealing with these five planning issues.

EXERCISE 15: DEFINE YOUR PLANNING ISSUES

Review the list of five planning issues presented in the preceding text and consider any others that are not mentioned. Document your planning issues in your Major Issues and Approaches for Resolution document (see Appendix A).

EXERCISE 16: DEFINE YOUR RESPONSE TO PLANNING ISSUES

For each planning issue you have identified in Exercise 15, develop a response using the examples presented in Table 5.5 or, as an alternative, define your own responses. Write these issue responses in your Major Issues and Approaches for Resolution document (see Appendix A).

TABLE 5.4 RESPONSE OPTIONS FOR PLANNING ISSUES

Issue 1. We don't have an agreed-upon common vision, focus, direction, goals, and objectives for the company—a business plan.

- Develop your business plan—the subject of this book.

Issue 2. We need a marketing and sales plan to target our markets, determine our entry strategies, and define our future products and services.

- Develop a marketing and sales plan.
- Acquire the services of an expert to support the development of this plan.

Issue 3. We're totally reactive; we don't plan strategically, tactically, or in any other way; we run by the seat of our pants.

- Develop and implement your business plan.

Issue 4. We don't implement the plans we do develop; we don't develop action plans as follow-on to our strategies; we lack the resources, accountability, and commitment (buy-in) to implement our plans.

- Manage your business plan to success (see Part 4).

Issue 5. We need a process to support the management and implementation of our plans.

- Manage your business plan to success (see Part 4).

 RESOURCES ISSUES AND RESPONSE OPTIONS

Resources issues address the need to acquire more staff, space, and equipment. As shown in Figure 5.5, 4 major resources issues were raised by the 20 sample companies. These issues ranged in frequency from 95 percent (19 companies raised the issue) to 30 percent (6 companies raised the issue). The leading resources issue, needing more staff, was the most popular single issue voiced in the entire 20-company survey. A brief statement of the four major resources issues follows:

1. *Need more staff (95 percent).* "We're understaffed; we need to expand our corporate (marketing and sales, human resources, accounting, contracts, financing, administration), line, and technical staff."

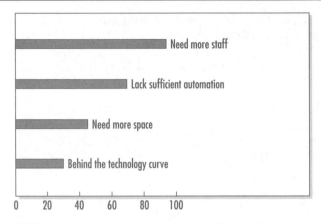

FIGURE 5.5 *Percentages of companies raising major resources issues.*

2. *Lack sufficient automation (70 percent).* "Our office automation and corporate network need expansion and enhancement."

3. *Need more space (45 percent).* "We're out of space; we need to expand or make more efficient use of our space. We need space for special activities, including a library, sales demonstration area, laboratory, proposal war room, and so on."

4. *Behind the technology curve (30 percent).* "We need to upgrade (or acquire) an e-mail system, get on the Internet, and develop an Internet homepage."

As previously mentioned, needing more staff is the most popular issue found in the 20-company sample. This issue can be resolved only if there are sufficient revenues available to make the necessary hires. As discussed in Chapter 4, hiring part-time employees or consultants to meet specific needs could be an interim solution if revenues don't warrant a full-time resource. Some of my clients who were lacking in sufficient revenue but saw the need to acquire staff immediately bit the bullet and raised the necessary capital through loans or investing from retained earnings. Others gave up a portion of their ownership to bring on senior staff. In most cases, this issue needs to be painfully set aside until the company can afford to take the necessary hiring actions.

After defining your resources issues in Exercise 17, identify means to eliminate these issues in Exercise 18. Table 5.5 presents response options for dealing with these four resources issues.

***EXERCISE 17:* DEFINE YOUR RESOURCES ISSUES**

Review the list of four resources issues presented in the preceding text and consider any others that are not mentioned. Document your resources issues in your Major Issues and Approaches for Resolution document (see Appendix A).

***EXERCISE 18:* DEFINE YOUR RESPONSE TO RESOURCES ISSUES**

For each resources issue you have identified in Exercise 17, develop a response using the examples presented in Table 5.5 or, as an alternative, define your own responses. Write these issue responses in your Major Issues and Approaches for Resolution document (see Appendix A).

 PERSONNEL SHORTAGES ARE TIED TO GROWTH

Most companies that are rapidly growing will periodically experience personnel shortages. As illustrated in Figure 5.6, as revenue grows, so does the workload, and there will always be shortages until the next wave of hiring takes place. I view this issue of needing more staff as healthy in most cases. For those companies that are not growing but are experiencing personnel shortages, management must look for means to increase efficiency instead of hiring more people.

END POINT

At this point, you have completed the first 18 exercises in identifying your function-specific

TABLE 5.5 RESPONSE OPTIONS FOR RESOURCES ISSUES

Issue 1.   We're understaffed; we need to expand our corporate (marketing and sales, human resources, accounting, contracts, financing, administration), line, and technical staff.

- Determine specific hiring requirements and develop budgets.
- Prioritize positions to be hired.
- Hire as soon as feasible.
- Consider hiring part-time and/or consultant staff.

Issue 2.   Our office automation and corporate network need expansion and enhancement.

- Determine requirements and develop a budget.
- Implement changes as soon as possible.

Issue 3.   We're out of space; we need to expand or make more efficient use of our space. We need space for special activities, including a library, sales demonstration area, laboratory, proposal war room, and so on.

- Determine requirements and develop a budget.
- Develop a floor plan.
- Retain a real estate agent and present requirements and preferences.

Issue 4.   We need to upgrade (or acquire) an e-mail system, get on the Internet, and develop an Internet homepage.

- Determine requirements and develop a budget.
- Implement changes as soon as possible.

and companywide issues and defining approaches to eliminate them. You will refer back to these issues and resolution approaches (described in your Major Issues and Approaches for Resolution document) later in Part 3 when you set out to define the near-term (tactical) objectives and actions in your business plan.

In identifying your own issues, you should have identified 10 to 45 issues and response approaches, but no more. If you have identified only several issues, consult others who are knowledgeable about your company and its issues, such as key employees or company advisors. Ask them what they view as issues or roadblocks in the way of your success. Open up your sights to the many dragons out there. The payoff to identifying and dealing with your

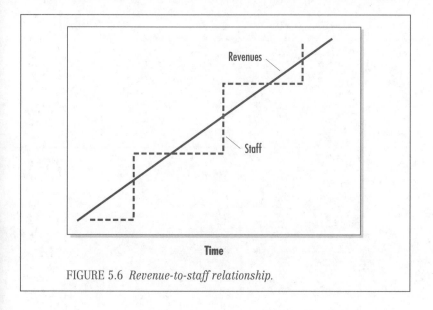

FIGURE 5.6 *Revenue-to-staff relationship.*

issues through the business plan is a major step toward increased performance for your company. Recall the quote from the beginning of Chapter 3: "Foolish are the generals who ignore the daily intelligence from the trenches." Enough said!

Develop the Plan

Begin with the end in mind.
—*Stephen Covey*

Step 1	Step 2	Step 3
Identify the issues	Develop the plan	Manage the plan

This part describes Step 2 of the planning process—developing the plan. Three chapters guide you through the complete development of your business plan. The approach incorporates discussion of each element of the plan—vision statement, mission statement, five-year goals, annual objectives, and the action plan—along with numerous examples to support you in completing the exercises presented throughout this part.

Chapter 6: Major Business Plan Elements presents an overview of the major elements of the business plan you will be developing.

Chapter 7: Develop Your Strategy leads you through the development of your vision statement, mission statement, and five-year goals.

Chapter 8: Define Your Tactics leads you through the development of your annual objectives and action plan.

Major Business Plan Elements

Make no little plans; they have no magic to stir men's blood. Make big plans, aim high in hope and work."

—*Daniel H. Burnham*

The second step of the planning process is to *develop the plan.* Having identified and documented the major issues facing your company and defined strategies to eliminate them in Part 2, you are now prepared to plan your future through the development of your business plan. As shown in Figure 6.1, the business plan contains the following five major elements:

1. *Vision statement.* Several words that draw a mental picture of your company, for example, General Electric's "Progress is our most important product" or Microsoft's "Where do you want to go today?"

2. *Mission statement.* A description of your company in 10 years—a definitive expansion of your vision statement.

3. *Five-year goals.* A snapshot of measurable results to be achieved in five years; reflects progress toward making your mission statement a reality.

4. *Annual objectives.* Objectives to be achieved by the end of the planning (fiscal) year in order to be on track toward achieving your five-year goals.

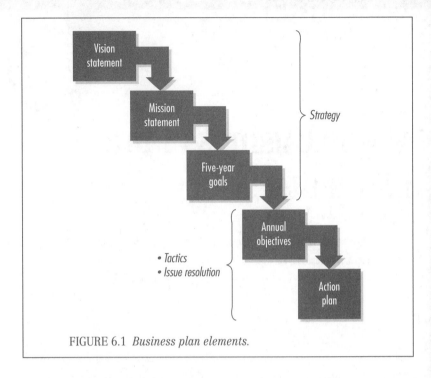

FIGURE 6.1 *Business plan elements.*

5. *Action plan.*   A list of near-term actions
   (30 to 45 days) in support of achieving your
   annual objectives.

KEY CONCEPT **STRATEGIC ELEMENTS**

   Referring to Figure 6.1, the first three
plan elements—vision statement, mission statement, and five-year goals—are strategic (longer
term) and serve as the basis for developing the
road map for your business. The *vision statement* presents, in just a few hard-hitting words,
your picture of your company. The *mission
statement* answers five questions about your
company. It's an expansion of your vision statement and puts in place your long-term, say
10-year, strategy for developing the kind of company you want to see in the future. The *five-
year goals* are clear and concise; in contrast to
your mission statement, they are measurable
milestones toward making your mission statement a reality. These three elements comprise
your strategy and set the stage for the development of the tactical part of your business plan.

KEY CONCEPT **TACTICAL ELEMENTS**

The last two plan elements shown in Figure 6.1—annual objectives and the action plan—are tactics (short-term) and are the vehicle for achieving your vision based on the road map the strategy provides. The *annual objectives* are highly measurable near-term milestones, typically to be achieved within a year. They can be considered as steps toward achieving your five-year goals. Finally, the *action plan* consists of near-term, say 30- to 45-day, activities to be undertaken to support achievement of the annual objectives. As shown in Figure 6.1, the resolution approach to the issues you've identified in Part 2 are described through the tactical activities you define in your annual objectives and supporting action plan.

KEY CONCEPT **THIS IS NOT YOUR FINAL PLAN**

It should be understood that the business plan you develop in this book is not to be thought of as being cast in concrete. It's an expression of the best strategies and supporting tactics you are able to define as of today. You should revisit your plan annually to review and modify your strategies (vision statement, mission statement, and five-year goals) based on a changing market and business environment or new insights or capabilities you possess. In addition, each year you will develop new tactics (next year's annual objectives and action plan) to support your previously defined strategies. Therefore, move forward with the development of your plan based on what you know today, but keep in mind that the plan will change in the future.

END POINT

The five major elements of the business plan are the vision statement, mission statement, five-year goals, annual objectives, and action plan. The remainder of Part 3 takes you through these five elements and includes examples to assist you in preparing each component of your business plan.

Appendix C presents an example of a completed business plan. This plan will give you a sense of what your final product will look like. This example business plan comes from one of my high-tech clients (the name of the company has been changed) who has been in business for over seven years and, as indicated by the numbers, is well on the way to creating a very successful company.

CHAPTER 7

Develop Your Strategy
The Vision Statement, Mission Statement, and Five-Year Goals

Nothing Happens Unless
First a Dream
        —Carl Sandburg

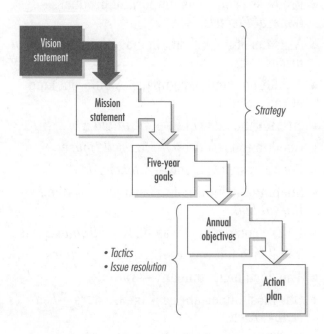

DEFINING THE VISION STATEMENT

K E Y CONCEPT

The vision statement is an attempt, in very few words, to paint a picture of your dream—your company in the minds of your customers, employees, and stakeholders. The term *stakeholders* include stockholders, your bank, and your suppliers—those relying on the success of your business. The purpose of the vision statement you will create in Exercise 19 is to motivate people and have them draw a positive inference from a few words describing your company. Make this vision statement a part of your logo; put it on your business cards, letterhead, business forms, documents, advertising, and public relations pieces.

The following is a sample list of vision statements, most of which you will recognize:

- Solutions for a small planet.—*IBM*
- For the life of your business.—*AT&T*
- Where do you want to go today?—*Microsoft*
- Coverage, Community, Commitment.—*WMAR-TV, Baltimore*
- Home of serious steaks.—*Ruth's Chris Steak House*
- I love what you do for me.—*Toyota*
- Progress is our most important product.—*General Electric*
- Artisans of the information age.—*RJO Enterprises*
- A different kind of company. A different kind of car.—*Saturn*
- Just for the taste of it.—*Coca-Cola*
- Good to the last drop.—*Maxwell House*
- For the way it's made.—*Kitchen Aid*
- Shaping the future of data communications.—*Digital Link*
- You've come a long way baby.—*Virginia Slims*
- You'll love the way we fly.—*Delta Airlines*
- The document company.—*Xerox*
- Our most important package is yours.—*Federal Express*
- You'll love the stuff we're made of.—*Pizza Hut*
- They make money the old fashioned way. They earn it.—*Smith Barney*

EXERCISE 19: CREATE A VISION STATEMENT

Review the list of vision statements presented in the preceding text to gain a sense of what companies are saying to the world about themselves. Develop several different vision statements for your company and write them on the cover of your business plan (see Appendix B). Share these candidate visions with others and get their comments and suggestions in order to finalize your vision statement.

WHAT YOUR VISION STATEMENT ACHIEVES

The vision statement, the business plan's first element, is a bold message directed toward your customers, employees, and stakeholders. It clearly and concisely expresses the vision of your company. The vision statement is the precursor to the next part of the plan—the mission statement.

 **DEVELOPING THE MISSION STATEMENT**

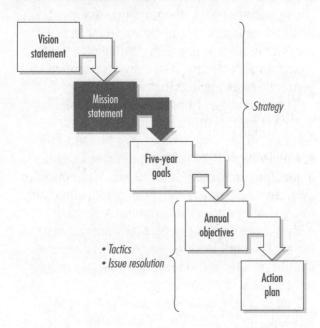

The mission statement is the second element of your business plan strategy. It is really the answer to the difficult question, "What business are you in?" This is the first question I ask my new or prospective clients, and it most often raises the response, "Now that's a good question." CEOs are typically too focused on the short-term, dealing with day-to-day issues, to really have a good idea as to where they are going. Somebody once said, "If you don't know where you are going, how will you know when you are lost?" Developing your mission statement gives you the opportunity to document, in a single page, a future picture of your company. It is the necessary roadmap for knowing where you're going, and, as Stephen Covey says, it enables you to "begin with the end in mind."

The mission statement is very strategic and describes your future company, typically 10 years from now. While some might think a 10-year time horizon is too long, given the rapidly changing business environment, keep in mind that you need to look far enough into the future to enable you to develop your long-term strategies. Recall that you will be revisiting your strategies each year and that you can make appropriate adjustments. In contrast to the rest of the business plan, the mission statement contains no numbers, no measurable factors; it's very qualitative. It is a very strategic view of your future company. It's really a statement of your values as applied to your company.

The challenge of developing an effective business plan centers on clearly framing a response to the question of what business you are in. Joseph R. Mancuso points out in his book *How to Start, Finance, and Manage Your Own Small Business* that "the importance of the question and its subsequent answer is widely accepted as the pivotal survival issue for every small businessperson."[1] The same should be said for medium and large businesses, as well.

For example, one need only look at IBM's missing the boat on the viability of the personal computer or the railroads' falling on their swords at the turn of the century when they chose to be in the railroad business instead of the transportation business. Peter F.

Drucker states in his classic book *Practice of Management* that "all companies which answer this question properly [what business are we in?] eventually succeed."[2] The mission statement is where you answer this critical question.

 ANSWERING THE FIVE CRITICAL MISSION STATEMENT QUESTIONS

The mission statement characterizes, in one page, your future company—say, 10 years from now. This is the time to do a little dreaming based on the realities of where you are today and where you believe you would like to go. The mission statement should answer the following five questions in order to describe what business your company is in:

1. Ten years from now, who are my clients and what am I selling?

2. Ten years from now, what value or benefit do my clients receive from my products and services?

3. Ten years from now, what special or unique characteristics of my products and services set me apart from the competition?

4. Ten years from now, what major marketing strategies do I employ to market and sell my products and services?

5. Ten years from now, what are my commitments to my clients, employees, and stakeholders?

How you answer each of these five very strategic questions will determine your company's direction and set the framework for the rest of your business plan. Recall that the mission statement is a picture of your company in the future. It's what you want your company to be—not necessarily an extension of what your business is today.

You may be familiar with mission statements that are much shorter than the one used here— two or three sentences. These are fine for displaying on your office walls and incorporating in your marketing materials, but they lack sufficlient detail to set the stage for setting goals and eventually developing your tactics. Your responses to the five questions will lay the foundation for an effective business plan. In order to help you frame your mission statement, examples taken from the mission statements of the 20 sample companies are provided.

Question 1: In 10 Years, Who Are My Clients and What Am I Selling?

The first mission statement question, which you'll answer in Exercise 20, deals with your future clients and what you'll be selling to them. This question gives you an opportunity to consider the possibility of future expansion of your products and services as well as your client base. For example, if your current client base is the federal government, do you believe you should expand in the future into state and local government or the commercial sector? Should your client base take on a global character? If you are strictly a product company, should you consider offering services in the future, or vice versa? It is acceptable, even encouraged, to be visionary regarding the business you will be in 10 years from now. Why put limits on a dream? Examples of responses to Question 1 follow:

1. The mission of ABC, Inc., is to provide our Fortune 500 Companies, government, and international clients with complete information system solutions, niche data management software products, specialized technology training, and expert advisory services.

2. The mission of DEF, Inc., is to provide our commercial, industrial, and government customers with waste and recycling products and services.

3. The mission of GHI, Inc., is to provide our mid-Atlantic construction, industrial, commercial, recycling, and homeowner customers with construction equipment and related products and services.

4. The mission of JKL Construction, Inc., is to profitably construct high-quality and energy-efficient custom residences.

5. The mission of MNO, Inc., a world-class provider of information technology solutions, is to provide our worldwide government, commercial, and consumer clients with networks, computer system integration, business process reengineering, and software development services and products.

Each of these five responses to the mission statement's first question clearly articulates the company's client base and the products and services it offers. Be assured that these five examples don't reflect the clients and offerings of these companies today, but are an expression of their *future* clients and offerings. As an example, company ABC serves only federal government clients today, but it plans to eventually expand its client base to include large private companies and international government and commercial organizations. Company MNO currently offers computer systems support, but, as indicated, it plans on considerably expanding its product and service line.

EXERCISE 20: DESCRIBE WHO YOUR CUSTOMERS ARE AND WHAT YOU'RE SELLING 10 YEARS FROM NOW

Review the five sample answers to Question 1 and document your own answer in your business plan (see Appendix B). Remember that this is the time to be a little aggressive; don't be tied to the clients and offerings your current company reflects. Describe what you think your products and services should be and what clients you should be serving 10 years from now.

Question 2: In 10 Years, What Value or Benefit Do My Clients Receive from My Products and Services?

The second mission statement question, which you'll answer in Exercise 21, deals with the benefits your clients will derive from your future offerings. It's important to understand what you want your future clients to get from doing business with you. What's their payoff? What will the nature of your products and services look like in order to maximize your client's benefit? Examples of responses to Question 2 follow:

1. The benefits our clients derive from our services are that they achieve their objectives better, faster, and more cost-effectively through innovative technological solutions.

2. The benefits of our products and services are that in an age of increasing environmental regulation, we provide our customers a single source for handling a broad array of waste-removal and recycling services and quality recycled products.

3. The benefits to our customers of our world-class products and customer-focused services are that they maximize production while minimizing downtime resulting in increased bottom-line profits."

4. The benefits our services and products provide to our clients are measurably increased productivity and performance and effective communications and decision making.

5. The benefits our services and products provide to our clients are expanded capabilities to accomplish their business missions, goals, and objectives.

EXERCISE 21: DESCRIBE THE VALUE OR BENEFITS YOUR CLIENTS WILL RECEIVE FROM YOUR PRODUCTS AND SERVICES 10 YEARS FROM NOW

Review the five sample answers to Question 2 above and document your own answer in your business plan (see Appendix B). Describe what benefits you think your products and services will offer to your clients in order for you to have a highly successful company 10 years from now. Think about the services and products you will be offering—place yourself in your client's shoes and answer the question, "How am I benefiting from your offerings?"

Question 3: In 10 Years, What Special or Unique Characteristics of My Products and Services Set Me Apart from the Competition?

In response to the third mission statement question, you will define what is unique or special about your company in Exercise 22. Why will clients purchase your products and services instead of your competition's? It's okay to be bold; remember, this is your dream you're describing. Examples of responses to Question 3 follow:

1. What distinguishes us from our competition is that we are a one-stop operation—the only source in the region providing the full life cycle of waste-handling and recycling services and products from hauling and disposal to processing, manufacturing, and consulting. In addition, we remain at the leading edge of the waste-recycling technology, and we maintain a constant focus on offering quality products and services and ensuring customer satisfaction.

2. What distinguishes us from our competition is our world-renowned product lines, our quality customer support, our state-of-the-art product-support facilities, and our high level of employee dedication and professionalism.

3. We outperform our competition because we maintain a currency with new and emerging construction methods and materials, the entire staff is oriented to paying attention to details, we are dedicated to a high-quality product, and we have a penchant toward achieving client satisfaction.

4. What differentiates us from our competition is our sound financial status, reputation for integrity, penchant for customer satisfaction, strong reputation in the marketplace, demonstrated performance on major programs, tightly focused business units, highly skilled technical staff, continuing investment in IR&D, high degree of executive availability, our willingness to change, and our highly creative solutions.

5. What distinguishes us from our competition is our proven track record, highly effective and motivated staff, ability to adapt to the constantly changing environment, high-end products that focus on the leading edge of technology, penchant for client satisfaction, development of niche capabilities, and our unique and proven tools and methodologies to optimize our client's investments.

EXERCISE 22: DESCRIBE THE SPECIAL OR UNIQUE CHARACTERISTICS OF YOUR PRODUCTS AND SERVICES THAT SET YOUR COMPANY APART FROM THE COMPETITION 10 YEARS FROM NOW

Review the five sample answers to Question 3 and document your own answer in your Business Plan (see Appendix B). Describe what you think will distinguish you from your competition, in order for you to have a highly successful company 10 years from now. Don't be hampered by the fact that you currently don't have any distinguishing characteristics. Remember, you have 10 years to get there, but don't wait. Setting yourself apart from your competition is perhaps one of the most critical strategies you need to implement in the short term.

Question 4: In 10 Years, What Major Marketing Strategies Do I Employ to Market and Sell My Products and Services?

In response to the fourth mission statement question, in Exercise 23 you'll describe marketing strategies that will make your company highly successful. Consider what the large companies in your market are doing and build from there. Don't limit yourself because of your notion of affordability. Remember, in 10 years you will be a successful company and will possess the personnel and financial resources necessary to carry out your strategies. Examples of responses to Question 4 follow:

1. Our major marketing strategies are to establish long-term client relationships, maintain a diversified client base, develop strategic busi-

ness alliances, maintain interorganizational marketing and sales synergy, actively participate in professional organizations, maintain high visibility in the marketplace, and make acquisitions to gain entry into selected market segments.

2. Our major marketing strategies are to obtain word-of-mouth referrals via our satisfied clients, obtain recognition in our industry and our marketplace via public relations, and aggressively pursue our niche market of high-quality custom homes.

3. Our major marketing strategies are to maintain a high visibility in the marketplace, continuously develop close relationships with key suppliers and large and small businesses in our market, continually maintain cognizance of emerging products, maintain strong client relationships, acquire companies that provide us market entry and expertise, and focus on developing our staff's expertise and professionalism.

4. Our major marketing strategies are to lock our customers in through the marriage of our information systems with theirs, providing the ultimate in customer service; to maintain a high visibility in the marketplace through continual development of strategic partners, nationwide advertising, and participation in professional, business, and community organizations; and to use our nationwide presence and our selected acquisitions to gain entry into niche markets.

5. Our major marketing strategies are to continuously expand business with current clients, develop and pursue niche markets, maintain high visibility in our marketplace, develop and maintain strategic relationships with both large and small companies, promote a business development culture throughout the company, research and evaluate bid opportunities to optimize marketing resources including early cultivation of potential clients, have a nationwide and international geographic presence, and acquire companies to provide entry into selected markets.

EXERCISE 23: DESCRIBE THE MAJOR MARKETING STRATEGIES YOU WILL EMPLOY TO MARKET AND SELL YOUR PRODUCTS AND SERVICES 10 YEARS FROM NOW

Review the five sample answers to Question 4 and document your own answer in your business plan (see Appendix B). Describe what you think your major marketing strategies should be in order to promote growth and have a highly successful company 10 years from now.

Question 5: In 10 Years, What Are My Commitments to My Clients, Employees, and Stakeholders?

In answering this fifth mission statement question in Exercise 24, you will define the relationship you will have with the three critical elements of your company—your customers, your employees, and your stakeholders. Setting your strategies in place for working with these three critical elements will put you in action toward achieving the mission of your company. Examples of responses to Question 5 follow:

1. We are committed to providing our clients with the highest-quality product at a fair price, our employees with an opportunity to grow both financially and professionally, and our stakeholders with the continued growth and profitability of the company.

2. We are dedicated to providing our clients with quality and value in supporting the achievement of their objectives, our employees with a rewarding and secure workplace and opportunity for their professional and financial growth, and our stakeholders with the continued growth and profitability of the company.

3. We are committed to providing our customers with courteous service and high-quality products and services at a competitive price under environmentally sound conditions, our employees with a safe and rewarding environment enabling career and financial growth, and our stakeholders

with the growth and profitability of the company.

4. We are committed to sustaining an excellent reputation with our customers, having our employees share in the company's vision and promoting their financial and professional growth, and providing to our stakeholders a company based on integrity and maintenance of a business strategy that ensures continued growth and profitability of the company.

5. We are committed to providing to our clients unsurpassed service and superior technical solutions, to our employees financial and professional growth in a fun place to work, and to our stakeholders continued growth and profitability of the company.

EXERCISE 24: DESCRIBE YOUR COMMITMENTS TO YOUR CUSTOMERS, EMPLOYEES, AND STAKEHOLDERS 10 YEARS FROM NOW

Review the five sample answers to Question 5 and document your own answer in your business plan (see Appendix B). Describe what you think you would like to commit to in terms of your clients, your employees, and your stakeholders. Recall that in addition to your clients and employees, other major stakeholders in your company include your bank or other financial backers; your suppliers, who rely upon your prompt payments for their goods and services; and, naturally, the stockholders or owners of your company.

WHAT YOUR MISSION STATEMENT ACHIEVES

A clear and concise corporate mission statement will ensure that you and the rest of the company's senior management understand and agree on the company's direction. It also serves to provide the company's employees with a clear and concise statement of the company's future from the perspective of its top management. The mission statement also provides the necessary focus for development of the next element of your plan—your five-year goals.

 **ESTABLISHING FIVE-YEAR GOALS**

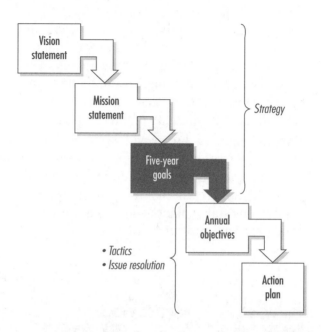

Bill Copeland says, "The trouble with not having a goal is that you can spend your life running up and down the field and never scoring." Five-year goals are a snapshot of your company five years from now—the basis for ensuring that you're not just running up and down the field. These are goals to be achieved by the end of the fifth fiscal year from your current planning year. They are meant to be measurable milestones to ensure that you're on the path towards making your mission statement a reality. That is to say, you need to set some quantifiable measures to be achieved 5 years from now for each point in your previously developed mission statement representing the state of the company 10 years from now. These five-year goals are like buoys guiding you to your destination—letting you know where you are going so you don't become lost along the way.

 Defining "Stretch" Goals

In setting your five-year goals, it is important to be realistic but not too conservative. Stretch a little and allow yourself the room to really make this company of yours an exciting and rewarding place to be five years from now. In deciding the proper level of goal setting, it is worthwhile to reflect on the previously cited David Hudson Burnham and what he suggested about goal setting at the turn of the century:

Make no little plans, they have no magic to stir men's blood.

In today's business world, which is reflective of participation by both genders, it's more appropriate to say, "no magic to stir *one's* blood." The point is, don't set five-year goals that are too easily achievable; they won't "stir your blood."

An example of stretching is in the setting of your five-year revenue goal. If you are currently a $2-million business, establishing a $3-million 5-year goal may be shooting too low. Considering inflation, this figure may not be large enough to instill excitement in you or your employees. Doubling in 5 years (approximately a 15 percent annual growth rate), resulting in a $4-million 5-year revenue goal, may be more appropriate. Note the use of the term *may be,* because your market, resources, and your own personal objectives need to become part of the equation.

Revenue Goals

The five-year revenue goal supports your mission statement's commitment to continued growth of the company. As an example, if you are a $5-million company today, setting a goal of $10 million in annual revenue in 5 years might be appropriate. This doubling in 5 years represents an average annual growth of approximately 15 percent. A more conservative annual growth rate of 10 percent would result in 60 percent growth ($8 million) in 5 years.

Your five-year revenue goal reflects your annual revenues (or in some cases, annual sales) at the end of the fifth year from the fiscal year in which you are writing the plan. For example, if you are writing this plan in your fiscal year 1999, the five-year goals should reflect performance in your fiscal year 2003. An example of a five-year revenue goal is as follows:

- Total annual revenues—$40 million by 2005
  By client area:

Fortune 500 companies	$18 million
Federal, state, and local government	$18 million
International	$4 million

  By business area:

Information systems	$20 million
Data management software products	$4 million
Specialized technology training	$8 million
Consulting (advisory services)	$8 million

In this example, the company provides computer system support services and products to its clients. Its 5-year $40-million revenue goal is expressed in two different ways: (1) by *client area*—who they will be selling to (large commercial companies, government organizations, and international companies and governments), and (2) by *business area*—what they will be selling (systems, products, training, and consulting). In addition to what you are selling, business areas might be represented as operating divisions of the company, separate geographic entities, or different product or service elements.

 **Defining Revenue Goals for Each Element of Your Business**

Breaking out the revenue among the various elements of your business (clients, product or service offerings, and departments or divisions) in Exercise 25 will help you determine how you need to grow your business. This is easier in larger companies, because departments or divisions typically do their own revenue breakouts; in smaller companies it might be more difficult to do. In a small company, you might want to set your revenue goals by defining revenues by product or service area.

For example, if you are in the photography business, you could break out the revenues by cameras and accessories, film sales and developing, and frames, albums, and other photographic accessories. If you are in the construction business, you could break the revenues out by remodeling and new home construction and by labor and materials. If you are in the computer business, you might break out your revenues by hardware sales, software sales, training, and consulting.

Another approach to setting a five-year revenue goal is to depict a specified growth rate, as follows:

- Achieve a compound annual sales growth of 25 percent per year through the next 5 years, resulting in a revenue of $15 million in 2005.
  By client area:
Commercial	$8 million
Industrial	$6 million
Government	$1 million

  By service or product area:
Waste-removal services	$7.5 million
Recycled products	$7.5 million

  By operating division:
Scrap	$5 million
Hauling	$5 million
Demolition	$5 million

In this case, the company is in the waste-removal and recycling business. Its 5-year $15-million revenue goal is expressed in three different ways: (1) by customers (commercial companies, industrial companies, and government organizations), (2) by service or product breakout (waste removal and recycled products), and (3) by what the company will be selling and how it will be organized (scrap, hauling, and demolition).

Notice that the five-year revenue goals in the two examples presented support two areas of the mission statement. First of all, they address the mission statement's first question of what the company is selling and who it is selling to; and second, the goal shows growth over the next five years supporting a portion of the fifth Mission Statement element—a growth commitment to the stakeholders.

> **EXERCISE 25: DESCRIBE YOUR FIVE-YEAR REVENUE GOALS**
>
> Review the two examples presented in the preceding text, and document your own five-year revenue goals in your business plan (see Appendix B). Select a total revenue goal and then break it out, as shown, by client area, business area, or any other way to portray some distinction in terms of where the revenues will come from. In developing your five-year revenue goals, refer to your earlier documented response to Question 1 on your mission statement, "Who are my clients and what am I selling?" This should provide the basis for the revenue breakout of your five-year goals.

KEY CONCEPT

Profit Goals

A second five-year goal should address profit—the major reason for companies to be in business. Some business owners are reluctant to state a profit goal in fear of giving their employees the impression that the boss is getting rich off of their efforts. Profits provide job security and professional and financial growth for your employees. In addition, your bankers demand a profitable company, profit helps capitalize the company, and profit is that pot of money to be spent on investments in the growth of your company. By all means, establish a profit goal.

Profit goals are typically presented in terms of pretax profits. Review your recent profit history and determine where you would like to be, within reason, in five years (Exercise 26). Refer to your previously defined revenue goal. Profit goals can be expressed in a number of different ways. Some examples of five-year profit goals follow:

- Total dollars—pretax income of $600,000
- Earnings before interest and taxes (EBIT)—achieve an EBIT of 11 percent
- Percentage of revenues—9 percent of revenues (pretax)
- By business element:
  Pretax profit by division:
Government	$6 million
Commercial	$2 million
International	$1.5 million

Pretax profit by products and services:
Products   25 percent
Services   12 percent

As shown here, the profit goal can be expressed in a number of ways, including total dollars, percentage of revenues, and dollars (or percentage of revenues) broken out by operating organization or products and services.

EXERCISE 26: DESCRIBE YOUR FIVE-YEAR PROFIT GOALS

Document your five-year profit goal in your business plan (see Appendix B). Define a goal for the entire company or, preferably, break it down by appropriate organizations (e.g., divisions, groups, and profit centers). As stated earlier, the profit goal, in dollars or percentage of revenue, is usually stated as income before taxes or before interest and taxes.

KEY CONCEPT   **Customer Satisfaction Goals**

You should have at least one goal reflecting client or customer satisfaction that addresses two areas of your mission statement: (1) the benefits of your products and services and (2) the commitment you make to your customers (Exercise 27). Some examples of client or customer satisfaction goals follow:

1. 95 percent customer satisfaction, as evidenced by surveys

2. 90 percent repeat business from previous year

3. 95 percent annual client retention rate

4. Client satisfaction evidenced by 90 percent repeat business in all market segments and 95 percent rating in client surveys

5. Monthly visits to client sites by all senior managers

The first example indicates that 5 years from now, the results of a customer survey of the company's performance will show that 95 percent of the customers are satisfied. The second and third examples indicate that in five years, a certain percentage of the clients on the books four years from now will still be customers in the fifth year. The fourth example combines both repeat business and survey results, and the fifth example incorporates a visit-the-client strategy. Needless to say, customer satisfaction is a critical objective and should show up in your list of five-year goals.

Another measure of customer satisfaction is customer retention rate, where a 5-year goal of 95 percent might be set. Here you are looking back at the end of your fifth year and determining what percentage of your past customers are still with you from the previous year.

EXERCISE 27: DESCRIBE YOUR FIVE-YEAR CUSTOMER SATISFACTION GOALS

Using the examples shown in the preceding text, and referring to the portion of your mission statement concerning customer satisfaction (customer benefits and customer commitment), document your five-year client satisfaction goal in your business plan (see Appendix B).

 Conducting Customer Surveys

Your mission statement most likely indicates that you are committed to customer satisfaction. As previously suggested, a 5-year goal that indicates a high level of customer satisfaction is 95 percent customer satisfaction, as evidenced by surveys. One way to measure the degree of customer satisfaction is to perform a customer survey. It is strongly suggested that you begin to conduct these surveys face-to-face with your customers. Mail or telephone surveys don't provide the necessary degree of personal concern.

Figure 7.1 presents an example of a survey form to support the information gathering. As indicated, the level of satisfaction is captured in a quantitative fashion in Question 1. The criteria shown can be changed to better match the products and services you provide. Questions 2 and 3 provide a qualitative response to how you are performing, and Questions 4 through 6 have a marketing focus. A reasonable 5-year goal for customer satisfaction might be 95 percent. In other words, on the average, your customers would give you a 95 percent satisfaction rating across the 6 criteria shown in Question 1 of Figure 7.1.

XYZ Corporation
Customer Survey

Date: _____

Organization: _____

Point of contact: _____

Telephone number: _____

1. Please rate, on a scale of 1 to 10 (1 is poor and 10 is outstanding), the provision of our services as follows:

- Quality   _____
- Responsiveness   _____
- Staff competency   _____
- Management competency   _____
- Technical capability   _____
- Cost   _____

2. What was the most significant benefit of our products and services in the past year?

_____

_____

_____

3. What recommendations do you have for us to better meet and exceed your expectations this year?

_____

_____

_____

4. If asked, would you provide a good reference for us and why?

_____

_____

_____

5. Are there any other services that you require that XYZ, Inc., might perform for you?

_____

_____

_____

6. Is there any other potential client that comes to mind who would benefit from our products and services?

_____

_____

FIGURE 7.1 *Customer survey form.*

Asking your clients how you are doing has two major benefits. First of all, you receive important feedback regarding your level of performance as perceived by your customer, and second, you have an opportunity to ask for more business. A happy client is the best lead for new business, and it's amazing how business will show up if you ask for it.

KEY CONCEPT   Competitive Distinction Goals

You should have one or two five-year goals supporting the answer to the third mission statement question, regarding what distinguishes you from your competition (Exercise 28). It's very important to develop these distinctions over the next five years because this will set you apart from your competitors and ensure your place in your market. You don't have to be the only company with these distinctions, but you want to be in the small group of companies ahead of the pack. Some examples of competitive distinction goals follow:

1. Three world-renowned product lines
2. 5 niche products generating 25 percent of the business
3. Three specialized training programs in place and all instructors fully certified in all training programs offered
4. Highly competitive rates, reflecting a 65 percent overhead and 6 percent G&A
5. Comprehensive R&D program in place leading toward new FY 2004 products and services
6. 20 certified engineers in niche technology areas
7. Good reputation in the marketplace, as evidenced by being on 10 major prime and 10 small business teams pursuing major ($25 million) programs
8. Highly experienced technical staff, as evidenced by average experience of 15 years

These examples of five-year goals all identify something that distinguishes the company from the competition.

EXERCISE 28: DESCRIBE YOUR FIVE-YEAR COMPETITIVE DISTINCTION GOALS

Using one or more of the examples shown in the preceding text, or other mission statement distinctions you have defined (distinguishing characteristics), document one or two five-year competitive distinction goals in your business plan (see Appendix B).

KEY CONCEPT **Strategic Marketing Goals**

You should have several goals supporting the answer to the fourth mission statement question, regarding what your major marketing strategies are (Exercise 29). It's very important to identify some measurable milestones toward achieving this critical element of your mission statement. Examples of major marketing strategy goals follow:

1. High visibility in the market, as evidenced by publishing 4 papers, actively participating in 5 professional organizations, participating in 3 trade shows, publishing 12 press releases, and advertising in 3 industry trade journals

2. Niche products generating half the company revenue

3. Advertising budget equal to 1.5 percent of gross revenues

4. Acquisition of two market-niche companies

5. 10 satellite offices—Richmond/Virginia Beach, Baltimore, Philadelphia, New York, San Francisco, San Diego, Los Angeles, Chicago, Denver, and Atlanta

6. $3-million revenue from team relationships with strategic alliance companies

7. Strategic alliances in place with five companies

8. Publishing a book on XYZ's best value methodology

These examples of five-year goals all identify marketing strategies that position the company for expanding its market share in the future.

EXERCISE 29: DESCRIBE YOUR FIVE-YEAR STRATEGIC MARKETING GOALS

Using one or more of the examples shown in the preceding text, or other mission statement marketing strategies you have identified (marketing strategies), document several five-year strategic marketing goals in your business plan (see Appendix B).

 **Employee Commitment Goals**

You should have one or two five-year goals supporting a portion of the answer to the fifth mission statement's question, regarding what your commitments are (Exercise 30). Examples of employee commitment goals follow:

1. Greater than 90 percent employee annual retention rate
2. Fully operational employee career progression plan in place
3. Performance-based compensation (PBC) plan in place
4. Employee profit-sharing program in place
5. Comprehensive management and staff training program in place
6. Employee ownership of the company in place
7. 6 percent 401(k) annual matching program in place

EXERCISE 30: DESCRIBE YOUR FIVE-YEAR EMPLOYEE COMMITMENT GOALS

Using one or more of the examples shown in the preceding text, or based on other mission statement employee commitments you have identified, document one or two five-year employee commitment goals in your business plan (see Appendix B).

RELATIONSHIP BETWEEN THE MISSION STATEMENT AND THE FIVE-YEAR GOALS

Your five-year goals should tie directly to your mission statement. To ensure that this has taken place, the development of your five-year goals has been framed with this in mind. Table 7.1 shows the relationship among the five elements of your mission statement and the five-year goals you have developed so far.

 **ADDITIONAL GOALS TO CONSIDER**

There are most likely some additional five-year goals that may not relate directly to the mission statement but do support the growth and profitability of your company and should be included in your list (Exercise 31). Examples of additional five-year goals follow:

1. Submit a total value of $10 million in proposals.
2. Submit 4 major ($10-million) competitive proposals as the prime contractor.
3. Establish a 35 percent competitive proposal win rate.
4. Enter FY 2004 with a backlog of $250 million.

TABLE 7.1 RELATIONSHIP OF MISSION STATEMENT QUESTIONS TO FIVE-YEAR GOAL EXERCISES

Question 1. In 10 years, who are my clients and what am I selling?
  Exercise 25: Describe Your Five-Year Revenue Goals

Question 2. In 10 years, what value or benefit do my clients receive from my products and services?
  Exercise 27: Describe Your Five-Year Customer Satisfaction Goals

Question 3. In 10 years, what special or unique characteristics of my products and services set me apart from the competition?
  Exercise 28: Describe Your Competitive Distinction Goals

Question 4. In 10 years, what major marketing strategies do I employ to market and sell my products and services?
  Exercise 29: Describe Your Five-Year Strategic Marketing Goals

Question 5. In 10 years, what are my commitments to my clients, employees, and stakeholders (e.g., stockholders, lenders, and vendors)?
  Exercise 25: Describe Your Five-Year Revenue Goals
  Exercise 26: Describe Your Five-Year Profit Goals
  Exercise 27: Describe Your Five-Year Customer Satisfaction Goals
  Exercise 30: Describe Your Five-Year Employee Commitment Goals

5. Create a prime contractor–to–subcontractor revenue ratio of 70/30.

6. Win all existing contract recompetes.

7. Establish a monthly productivity by division of:

Scrap	3,000 tons
Hauling	2,000 loads
Demolition	15,000 tons

8. Establish a workforce of 250 full-time employees.

9. Be active in local college recruiting.

10. Own our headquarters building.

11. Establish a board of directors and meet quarterly.

12. Hire senior staff to ensure a complete corporate infrastructure is in place—marketing and sales, human resources, finance, accounting, and administration.

The first four additional goals listed here focus on business-development activity in support of the revenue goals described earlier and are important metrics in ensuring that the business pipeline is constantly filled. The fifth goal is a means of ensuring that a company is in control of its business as a prime contractor, as opposed to being at the mercy of other companies as a subcontractor.

The sixth goal addresses the fact that you want to win all recompeted contracts where you were the incumbent contractor. The seventh goal is a productivity goal that supports both revenue and profit goals. Productivity goals are important, and you should consider including them in your list. The remaining five additional goals are self-explanatory, and several may be appropriate for your company.

EXERCISE 31: DESCRIBE ANY ADDITIONAL FIVE-YEAR GOALS

Using one or more of the examples shown in the preceding text, or based on other five-year goals you may feel are appropriate, document any additional five-year goals in your business plan (see Appendix B).

WHAT YOUR FIVE-YEAR GOALS ACHIEVE

Your five-year goals stem from your mission statement and are quantifiable steps toward its achievement. They are the final strategic element of your plan and form the basis for defining your tactical annual objectives.

END POINT

With the development of your strategy—your vision statement, mission statement, and five-year goals—you have now completed the first three elements of your business plan. Your strategy is the long-term underpinnings of your company or organization. With this roadmap in hand, it's time to develop the necessary tactics, or short-term activities (annual objectives and action plan), to begin implementing your strategies. The five-year goals you have just developed will provide an appropriate basis for developing the next plan element, annual objectives, in Chapter 8.

CHAPTER 8

Define Your Tactics
Annual Objectives
and the Action Plan

The end justifies the means.
—H. Busenbaum

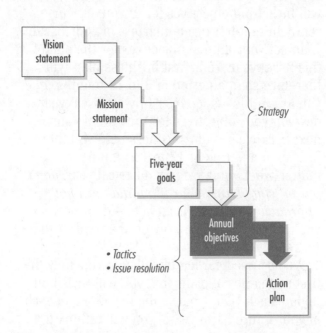

KEY CONCEPT

SETTING ANNUAL OBJECTIVES

With the annual objectives and action plan (your tactics) in hand, your company can begin to define the *means* that must be undertaken to achieve the *end* (your strategy). The annual objectives stem directly from each of the five-year goals you developed in Chapter 7 and identify what has to be achieved by the end of this fiscal year in order to be on track with your five-year goals. A five-year goal may produce multiple annual objectives. Objectives need to be specific, measurable, and somewhat aggressive but realizable milestones on the way toward meeting your five-year goals.

 **ESTABLISHING A PLANNING TIMEFRAME**

Annual objectives reflect both quantitative and qualitative milestones for the company that must be achieved in order to have a good year and support the eventual attainment of your five-year goals. In developing your annual objectives, you must determine the year you will be setting objectives for. If you are currently in the first three-quarters of your fiscal year, set your annual objectives for the end of this fiscal year. Your first business plan will therefore span a period of 3 to 12 months. If you are in the last quarter of your fiscal year, develop your objectives for the end of your next fiscal year; your business plan will therefore span a period of 12 to 15 months. No matter where you are in your fiscal year, *don't put off completing your planning until you approach your next fiscal year*—do it now so you can put your company on the road to success today.

As discussed earlier, this plan is hopefully the first in a series of plans that you will revisit and update each year. Prior to the beginning of each of your future fiscal years, you will rethink the strategy you developed in Chapter 7 (vision statement, mission statement, and five-year goals), make any necessary changes stemming from internal or external business stimuli, and develop a new set of annual objectives and a new action plan for the coming year. The important thing is to develop the plan now and get in synch with your fiscal year at your next planning session.

K E Y CONCEPT

ESTABLISHING ACCOUNTABILITY

For all but the smallest companies, achieving the annual objectives is not the CEO's responsibility alone. Other senior line and staff managers must take on this responsibility, as well. Holding all executives accountable to these annual objectives is an excellent basis for assessing their performance and is what *management by objectives* is all about. (Management by objectives is discussed in more detail in Part 4.)

Each annual objective needs a champion to take on the responsibility for achieving it. If you are a sole proprietor or you run a small business with just a few employees, there may not be anyone else to take on the responsibility for the annual objectives. If your company has employees, consider assigning them at least a portion of an annual objective or two in order to give them a direct hand in the future success of the company. I have often been surprised at the results from previously untried personnel—one of them could be a future vice president.

For example, assume a company gross revenue objective of $10 million. In this case, each operating director (department head, division director, etc.) may be assigned—or, better yet, volunteer—to take on a certain revenue figure whose sum, for all operating elements of the company, meets or exceeds the company's $10-million objective. In turn, each operating element should use its objective as the basis for assigning targets to various subelements of the operating organization, and so on throughout the organization. This approach of decomposing company targets and assigning them to the various line and staff organizations is an effective means of monitoring company performance and evaluating key personnel.

K E Y CONCEPT

REVENUE OBJECTIVES

Just as you developed five-year revenue goals in Exercise 25, you should have annual revenue objectives, as well (Exercise 32). Table 8.1 provides a comparison of a five-year rev-

TABLE 8.1 EXAMPLE OF A FIVE-YEAR REVENUE GOAL AND A RELATED ANNUAL REVENUE OBJECTIVE

Five-Year Goal: Total Revenues, $40 Million	Annual Objective: Total Revenues, $19 Million (T. Boss)
By Client Area	
Fortune 500 companies, $18 million	Fortune 500 companies, $2 million (J. Smith)
Federal, state, and local government, $18 million	Federal, state, and local government, $17 million (T. Jones)
International, $4 million	No international objective
By Business Area	
Information Systems, $20 million	Information systems, $10 million (T. Jones)
Data management software products, $4 million	Data management software products, $0.6 million (W. Stephans)
Specialized technology training, $8 million	Consulting (advisory services), $9.4 million (M. Wells)
Consulting (advisory services), $8 million	No specialized technology training objective

enue goal and an annual revenue objective. Notice that each annual objective has a *champion* (names in parentheses)—the person responsible for achieving each stated objective.

The company in Table 8.1 has a $40-million five-year revenue goal. It can be seen that it plans to approximately double this year's revenues in five years. The annual revenue objective comes directly from the five-year revenue goal in terms of being broken out by client area and business area. Comparing the five-year goal and the annual objective, the following can be seen for this year's objective: (1) The company is primarily a government contractor, although it is beginning to move out in the commercial arena; (2) the company doesn't plan to enter the international market this year; and (3) the data management software products business area is still in the formative stage, with significant growth planned over the next five years. In addition, the company does not plan to initiate a thrust in the specialized training business area in the coming year.

DEVELOPING A REVENUE PROJECTION

In setting your annual revenue objective for the current (or approaching) fiscal year, you should develop an annual revenue projection to serve as a basis for setting your targets. For most manufacturing and service businesses, this projection should reflect contracts or orders already received, orders underway but not yet received, proposals submitted but not yet awarded, proposals being developed but not yet submitted, and leads identified but not yet moved to the order or request for proposal stage, as well as any other category of potential sale that is applicable to your business. Apply probability percentages to each of these categories (e.g., existing contracts, 100 percent; orders underway, 70 percent; outstanding proposals, 30 percent) in order to arrive at a factored forecast that more realistically reflects or approximates reality. Figure 8.1 presents an example of a 12-month sales (or revenue) projection where the monthly sales range from $100,000 to $150,000. Figure 8.2 shows the cumulative sales projection; as indicated, the company expects to exceed $1.5 million over the projected 12-month period.

If the targeted fiscal year is just beginning and your factored forecast shows revenues of $5 million, you may want to set your revenue objective higher than this number (depending on the nature of the business and how far you want to stretch), because you have 12 months to identify and acquire new business. On the other

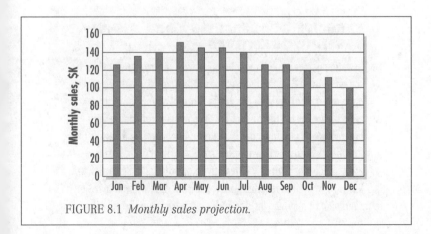

FIGURE 8.1 *Monthly sales projection.*

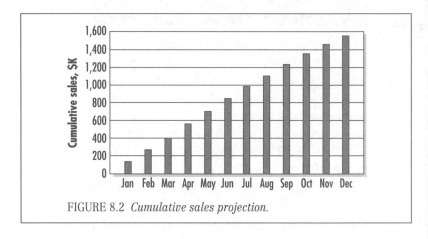

FIGURE 8.2 *Cumulative sales projection.*

hand, if your factored sales forecast shows $1 million and the typical period from lead identification to a final sale is 9 months, you should probably not target much more than $1 million.

In contrast to the manufacturing and service business area, where specific contracts or business opportunities can be identified, revenue forecasting for the wholesale or retail business takes on another set of factors dealing with historical data, new lines, new locations, and other considerations. Independent of the type of business you are in, it's important to project your revenues over the planning fiscal year to have a realistic basis for setting your revenue and sales objectives. I am not suggesting that annual revenue objectives be tied directly to your revenue projection. The revenue projection can be considered more or less in the bag, whereas you want your annual objectives to be somewhat more aggressive.

EXERCISE 32: DESCRIBE YOUR ANNUAL REVENUE OBJECTIVES

In defining your annual revenue objectives, review the example presented in Table 8.1, the five-year revenue goals you defined earlier, and your annual revenue projection. Document your own annual revenue objectives for the current (or upcoming) fiscal year in your business plan (see Appendix B). Select a total revenue objective and then break it out, as shown in Table 8.1, by client area, business area, product area or any other way to portray some distinction in terms of where the revenues will come from. Don't forget to assign a *champion* (it may be you) for each of your revenue objectives.

KEY CONCEPT   PROFIT OBJECTIVES

Just as you developed five-year profit goals, you should have annual profit objectives (Exercise 33). In setting your profit objective for the current (or approaching) fiscal year, review your recent profit history and your most recent income statement—also called a *profit and loss* (P&L) statement. The income statement provides a picture of the company's profitability. Table 8.2 presents an example of an income statement for a $5-million company. Note that operating income is referred to as *earnings before interest and taxes* (EBIT) and profit is referred to as *net income.* The current (1999) and previous (1998) years are presented for comparison and, as indicated, sales have increased 18 percent and profits 22 percent—a relatively good year.

With the profit history and your five-year profit goals as a baseline, this year's profit objective might take the form of one of the examples shown in Table 8.3, which presents examples of five-year profit goals and associated annual profit objectives.

As Table 8.3 shows, the annual profit objective can be expressed in a number of ways, including dollars, percentage of revenues, and

TABLE 8.2 SAMPLE INCOME STATEMENT, $K

Income Statement	1999	1998
Gross income (sales)	$5,000	$4,250
Less cost of goods sold	(3,625)	(3,110)
Gross profit	1,375	1,140
Gross margin	27.5%	26.8%
Expenses		
Sales and marketing	595	485
General and administrative	175	160
Less depreciation	95	85
Total expenses	865	730
Operating income (EBIT)	510	410
Interest charges	85	62
Income before taxes	425	348
Taxes @ 35%	149	122
Net income	$ 276	$ 226

TABLE 8.3 EXAMPLES OF FIVE-YEAR PROFIT GOALS AND RELATED ANNUAL PROFIT OBJECTIVES

Five-Year Goal	Annual Objective
Achieve a pretax income of $600,000.	Achieve a pretax income of $50,000 (T. Mann).
Achieve an EBIT of 11%.	Achieve an EBIT of 8% (P. Katz).
By Division	
Government, $1 million.	Government, $100,000 (L. Brown).
Commercial, $500,000.	Commercial, $50,000 (J. James).
International, $100,000.	No international objective.

dollars or percentage of revenues by operating organization. Notice that for the three examples in Table 8.3, the profit objective is smaller than the five-year profit goal because most companies expect to see increased revenues and profits in the future. Notice also that the company that broke its profit out by operating division showed a five-year profit goal stemming from an international division, whereas the annual profit objective reflects that the division has not yet gotten off the ground.

EXERCISE 33: DESCRIBE YOUR ANNUAL PROFIT OBJECTIVES

Define your annual profit objective by reviewing the examples presented in Table 8.3, the five-year profit goals you developed earlier, and your projected income statement. Document your own profit objectives for the current (or upcoming) fiscal year in your business plan (see Appendix B). As shown in Table 8.3, you may desire to break the profit objective down by operating organization, business area, or by some other more appropriate distinction. Don't forget to assign a *champion* (it may be you) for each of your profit objectives.

CUSTOMER SATISFACTION OBJECTIVES

Your customer satisfaction annual objectives (Exercise 34) will stem from the five-year customer satisfaction goals you previously developed. Using the five-year customer satisfaction goals you developed earlier as a baseline, this year's customer satisfaction objectives might include those shown in Table 8.4.

Referring to the five-year customer satisfaction goals in Table 8.4, it can be seen that the level of customer satisfaction for annual objectives is somewhat reduced as compared to the five-year goals. This is due to the fact that you may be putting some new customer satisfaction process in place, resulting in a less aggressive set of objectives. Remember that the annual

---

EXERCISE 34: **DESCRIBE YOUR CUSTOMER SATISFACTION ANNUAL OBJECTIVES**

In defining your annual customer satisfaction objectives, review the examples presented in Table 8.4 and the five-year customer satisfaction goals you developed earlier. Document your own customer satisfaction annual objectives for the current (or upcoming) fiscal year in your business plan (see Appendix B). Don't forget to assign a *champion* (it may be you) for each of your customer satisfaction objectives.

TABLE 8.4 EXAMPLES OF FIVE-YEAR CUSTOMER SATISFACTION GOALS AND RELATED ANNUAL CUSTOMER SATISFACTION OBJECTIVES

Five-Year Goal	Annual Objective
95% customer satisfaction, as evidenced by surveys	85% customer satisfaction, as evidenced by surveys
90% repeat business	80% repeat business
95% annual client retention	80% annual client retention
Client satisfaction evidenced by 90% repeat business in all market segments and 95% rating in client surveys	Client satisfaction evidenced by 80% repeat business in all market segments and 85% rating in client surveys
Monthly visits to client sites by all senior managers	Visits to client sites by CEO at least twice a year

objectives are steps along the way toward
achieving your five-year goals.

 ### COMPETITIVE DISTINCTION OBJECTIVES

Again, your competitive distinction annual objectives (Exercise 35) should come from your five-
year competitive distinction goals. Using the
five-year competitive distinction goals you developed earlier as a baseline, this year's competitive
distinction objectives might include those shown
in Table 8.5. Comparing the competitive distinction annual objectives with the competitive distinction five-year goals in Table 8.5, it can be
seen that the objectives defined are steps along
the way toward achieving the goals.

**EXERCISE 35: DESCRIBE YOUR
COMPETITIVE DISTINCTION ANNUAL
OBJECTIVES**

In defining your annual competitive distinction objectives, review the
examples presented in Table 8.5 and the five-year competitive distinction goals you developed earlier. Document your own competitive
distinction objectives in your business plan (see Appendix B). Don't
forget to assign a *champion* (it may be you) for each of your competitive distinction objectives.

 ### STRATEGIC MARKETING OBJECTIVES

Your strategic marketing annual objectives (Exercise 36) stem from the five-year strategic marketing goals you developed earlier. Using these
five-year strategic marketing goals as a baseline,
this year's strategic marketing objectives might
include those shown in Table 8.6. Again, comparing these examples of strategic marketing objectives with their counterparts in the five-year
goals, it can be seen that the objectives are steps
along the way toward achieving the goals.

TABLE 8.5 EXAMPLES OF FIVE-YEAR COMPETITIVE DISTINCTION GOALS AND RELATED ANNUAL COMPETITIVE DISTINCTION OBJECTIVES

Five-Year Goal	Annual Objective
Three world-renowned product lines	One world-renowned product line in place or a plan in place to create a world-renowned product line in the next fiscal year
5 niche products generating 25% of the business	2 niche products generating 10% of the business or plan in place to offer a niche product in the next fiscal year
Three specialized training programs in place and all instructors fully certified in all training programs offered	Specialized training program in place and half the instructors fully certified in all training programs offered
Highly competitive rates, reflecting a 65% overhead and 6% G&A	Highly competitive rates, reflecting a 75% overhead and 8% G&A
Comprehensive R&D program in place leading toward new FY 2004 products and services	R&D program plan in place for FY 2000
20 Certified engineers in niche technology areas	3 certified engineers in niche technology areas
Good reputation in the marketplace, as evidenced by being on 10 major prime and 10 small business teams pursuing major ($25-million) programs	Good reputation in the marketplace, as evidenced by being on a major prime and a small business team pursuing major ($15-million) programs
Highly experienced technical staff, as evidenced by average experience of 15 years	10-year average experience of technical staff

EXERCISE 36: DESCRIBE YOUR STRATEGIC MARKETING ANNUAL OBJECTIVES

In defining your annual strategic marketing objectives, review the examples presented in Table 8.6 and the five-year strategic marketing goals you developed earlier. Document your own strategic marketing objectives for the current (or upcoming) fiscal year in your business plan (see Appendix B). Don't forget to assign a *champion* (it may be you) for each of your strategic marketing objectives.

TABLE 8.6 EXAMPLES OF FIVE-YEAR STRATEGIC MARKETING GOALS AND RELATED ANNUAL STRATEGIC MARKETING OBJECTIVES

Five-Year Goal	Annual Objective
High visibility in the market, as evidenced by publishing 4 papers, actively participating in 5 professional organizations, participating in 3 trade shows, publishing 12 press releases, and advertising in 3 industry trade journals.	Gain visibility in the market, as evidenced by publishing one paper, actively participating in a professional organization, participating in a trade show, publishing four press releases, and advertising in an industry trade journal.
Niche products generating half the company revenue.	Niche products generating 20% of the company revenue.
Advertising budget equal to 1.5% of gross revenues.	Develop an advertising budget for next fiscal year.
Acquisition of two market-niche companies.	Identify one possible acquisition.
10 Satellite offices—Richmond/ Virginia Beach, Baltimore, Philadelphia, New York, San Francisco, San Diego, Los Angeles, Chicago, Denver, and Atlanta.	Open first satellite office in Baltimore.
$3-million revenue from teaming relationships with strategic alliance companies.	Submit a proposal with a strategic partner.
Strategic alliances in place with five companies.	(None.)
Publishing a book on XYZ's best value methodology.	Identify the subject matter for a book and develop a first-cut outline.

EMPLOYEE COMMITMENT OBJECTIVES

Your employee commitment annual objectives (Exercise 37) stem from the five-year employee commitment goals you developed earlier. Using these five-year employee commitment goals as a baseline, this year's employee commitment objectives might include those shown in Table 8.7.

EXERCISE 37: DESCRIBE YOUR EMPLOYEE COMMITMENT ANNUAL OBJECTIVES

In defining your annual employee commitment objectives, review the examples presented in Table 8.7 and the five-year employee commitment goals you developed earlier. Document your own employee commitment annual objectives for the current (or upcoming) fiscal year in your business plan (see Appendix B). Don't forget to assign a *champion* (it may be you) for each of your employee commitment objectives.

 ADDITIONAL ANNUAL OBJECTIVES TO CONSIDER

You may have identified additional five-year goals that support the growth and profitability of your company. Using the additional five-year goals you might have developed earlier as a baseline, additional annual objectives (Exercise 38) might include those shown in Table 8.8.

TABLE 8.7 EXAMPLES OF FIVE-YEAR EMPLOYEE COMMITMENT GOALS AND RELATED ANNUAL EMPLOYEE COMMITMENT OBJECTIVES

Five-Year Goal	Annual Objective
Greater than 90% employee annual retention rate	80% employee annual retention rate
Fully operational employee career progression plan in place	(None)
Performance-based compensation (PBC) plan in place	Employee position descriptions developed and FY 2000 objectives defined
Employee profit-sharing program in place	Profit-sharing study completed
Comprehensive management and staff training program in place	All senior managers to attend one professional training program
Employee ownership of company in place	Stock distribution study completed
6% 401(k) annual matching program in place	Nonmatching 401(k) program in place

EXERCISE 38: DESCRIBE YOUR ADDITIONAL ANNUAL OBJECTIVES

In defining any additional annual objectives, review the examples presented in Table 8.8 and the five-year additional goals you might have developed earlier. Document your own additional objectives for the current (or upcoming) fiscal year in your business plan (see Appendix B). Don't forget to assign a *champion* (it may be you) for each of your additional objectives.

 **ANNUAL OBJECTIVES STEMMING FROM ISSUES**

As discussed in Chapter 3, the issues and resolution strategies you defined in Chapters 4 and 5 need to be incorporated into the business plan through tactical near-term actions. Most issues should be addressed immediately through the action plan discussed in following sections. Some issues can be addressed only by setting their elimination as an annual objective rather than addressing them in the short run (Exercise 39). Some examples of annual objectives stemming from the 8 predominant issues voiced by the 20 sample companies (as discussed in Chapter 3) are shown in Table 8.9.

EXERCISE 39: DESCRIBE ANNUAL OBJECTIVES THAT STEM FROM YOUR COMPANY'S ISSUES

In defining the annual objectives stemming from your issues, review your list of issues defined earlier in your Major Issues and Approaches for Resolution document, select those that you believe warrant longer-term solutions, and set them as annual objectives. Document the current (or upcoming) fiscal year objectives stemming from these issues in your business plan (see Appendix B). Don't forget to assign a *champion* (it may be you) for each of the objectives stemming from your previously defined issues.

WHAT YOUR ANNUAL OBJECTIVES ACHIEVE

Your annual objectives serve as the milestones for successfully implementing your business plan. The objectives stem from your five-year goals and are quantifiable and tactical steps

TABLE 8.8 EXAMPLES OF ADDITIONAL FIVE-YEAR GOALS AND RELATED ANNUAL OBJECTIVES

Five-Year Goals	Annual Objectives
Submit $10 million (total value) in Proposals.	Submit $1.5 million (total value) in proposals.
Submit 4 major ($10 million) competitive proposals as the prime contractor.	Submit one proposal as the prime contractor.
35% competitive proposal win rate	Win one competitive proposal.
Enter FY 2004 with a backlog of $250 million.	Enter FY 2000 with a backlog of $20 million.
Create a prime contractor–subcontractor revenue ratio of 70/30.	Create a prime contractor–subcontractor revenue ratio of 40/60.
Win all existing contract recompetes.	Win 50% of contract recompetes.
Establish a monthly productivity by division of: Scrap, 3,000 tons Hauling, 2,000 loads Demolition, 15,000 tons	Establish monthly productivity by division of: Scrap, 2,000 tons Hauling, 1,500 loads Demolition, 3,000 tons
Establish a workforce of 250 employees.	Establish a workforce of 100 employees.
Be active in local college recruiting.	Have local college recruitment plan in place for 2000.
Own our headquarters building.	Sign lease for expanded office space.
Establish a board of directors and meet quarterly.	Develop a list of potential board members.
Have a complete corporate infrastructure in place—marketing and sales, HR, finance, accounting, and administration.	Hire a director of marketing and sales.

toward the eventual achievement of the strategies you defined in Chapter 7. You will be tracking your performance against your annual objectives throughout the year.

At this point you have completed the fourth element of your business plan—your annual objectives. The remaining activity is to develop an action (or implementation) plan that serves

TABLE 8.9 EXAMPLES OF ANNUAL OBJECTIVES THAT STEM FROM ISSUES

Issue 1. Our approach to business development is haphazard and uncoordinated; everybody's doing their own thing. There are no standard business-development practices and procedures in place.
  Objective. A corporatewide business-development process and associated procedures are in place and fully operational.

Issue 2. We're not rewarding our effective employees sufficiently; we lack management and staff incentives such as a performance-based compensation program and/or a stock-ownership/profit-sharing plan.
  Objective. A companywide performance-based compensation program is in place and fully operational.

Issue 3. We don't sufficiently train our management and staff.
  Objective. An employee training program is fully defined and in place for implementation next year.

Issue 4. There are communication gaps between major elements of our company; between line organizations, between staff organizations, and between line and staff.
  Objective. A program for regularly scheduled line and staff meetings is defined and meetings are underway; additional communications enhancements are defined for implementation next year.

Issue 5. Our managers don't understand their roles, responsibilities, and authorities to carry out their jobs; there's no clear statement of goals and objectives; and we lack position/job descriptions.
  Objective. All members of the management staff have position descriptions and objectives defined for next fiscal year; a plan for implementing position descriptions for all employees is in place for implementation next year.

Issue 6. We lack standardized, documented, and effective systems, processes, policies, and procedures; we shoot from the hip.
  Objective. A preliminary set of company policies and procedures is in place; a survey of required systems and processes is completed; and a program for implementation is developed for next year.

Issue 7. We don't have an agreed-upon common vision, focus, direction, goals, and objectives for the company—a business plan.
  Objective. This year's business plan is fully implemented and next year's plan is in place.

Issue 8. We're understaffed; we need to expand our corporate (marketing/sales, human resources, accounting, contracts, financing, administration) and line/technical/operations staff.
  Objective. Near-term "must hires" are on staff and a full staffing plan is in place for next year.

to describe the necessary near-term actions to support achievement of your annual objectives.

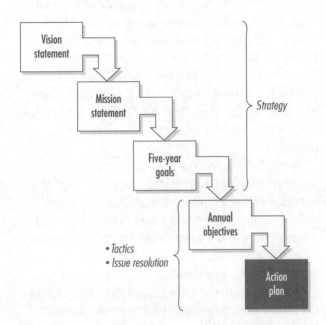

DEFINING THE ACTION PLAN

William Jennings Bryan said that "Destiny is not a matter of chance, it is a matter of choice; it is not a thing to be waited for, it is a thing to be achieved." In terms of the business plan, your destiny can be achieved only if you are able to define the necessary near-term actions (say, 30 to 45 days) you and your staff will take to begin the attainment of your annual objectives. This is where the rubber meets the road in terms of implementing your business plan.

The action plan consists of a set of action items that describe the first things to be done toward (1) meeting each annual objective you defined in your business plan, and (2) addressing each issue you identified in your list of issues and issue-response strategies. Each action item describes what will be done, by whom, and when it will be completed.

Action Items Stemming from Annual Objectives

A portion of the action plan's action items comes directly from your annual objectives.

That is to say, for each objective, what's the first thing you need to do to begin accomplishing the stated objective? When a particular action item is completed, the appropriate question to ask next is, "What is the next necessary action to take toward achieving a particular annual objective?" In other words, your action plan is never completed for a given planning year until each objective is attained. The action plan defines the steps along the way toward achieving your objectives.

Table 8.10 provides examples of annual objectives (with each champion noted) and the corresponding action items. As shown, each action item contains the three critical items of what's going to be accomplished, who's responsible for accomplishing it, and the date the action will be completed.

For example, the first action item to support the $2-million revenue objective is to develop a list of Fortune 500 companies with headquarters in the Boston area. When this list is compiled, the next action item might be to set up meetings with the Boston-area companies to present your credentials. Later action items might be to meet with additional personnel from those companies or perhaps to submit a proposal to deliver a product or a service. As dis-

TABLE 8.10 EXAMPLES OF ANNUAL OBJECTIVES AND RELATED ACTION ITEMS

Objectives	Action Items
1. Total revenues, $19 million (C. Boss).	1. T. Smith: Develop a list of Fortune 500 companies with headquarters in the Boston area by 4/5/00.
By client area: Fortune 500 companies, $2 million (T. Smith).	2. D. Barnes: Follow up with Prudential and Travelers insurance re recent capabilities briefings by 4/12/00.
Federal, state, and local government, $17 million (T. Jones).	3. T. Jones: Submit Air Force proposal on 4/28/00.
	4. T. Jones: Contact M. McHearn (HUD) re briefing date by 5/1/00.

TABLE 8.10 *(Continued)*

Objectives	Action Items
	5. F. Thompson: Set up meet with N. Niles (USDA) re sales call by 4/19/00.
2. Achieve an EBIT of 8% of revenues (C. Boss).	6. J. Cash: Close March books by 4/15/00 and determine year-to-date profit.
3. 85% customer satisfaction, as evidenced by surveys (T. Jones/T. Smith).	7. L. Lewis: Develop customer satisfaction survey instrument by 4/21/00.
4. R&D program plan in place for 2001 (H. Fields).	8. H. Fields: Survey engineering department re potential R&D programs by 5/15/00.
5. Two niche products generating 10% of the business (S. Sales).	9. S. Sales: Develop marketing plan for new network and database products by 5/1/00.
6. Participate in two trade shows (K. Burns).	10. K. Burns: Review fall season trade shows and make a recommendation to the CEO by 4/15/00.
7. All senior managers attend one professional training program (H. Caring).	11. A. Crane: Identify three senior manager training-program candidates and brief senior staff team by 5/1/00.
8. Sign lease for expanded office space (C. Boss).	12. P. Stephans: Set up meeting with Jones Real Estate by 5/12/00.
9. Hire a director of marketing and sales (C. Boss).	13. C. Craft: Place newspaper ad for marketing and sales director by 4/15/00.
10. Companywide performance-based compensation program is in place and fully operational (R. Taylor).	14. R. Taylor: Set up meeting with K. Kames (compensation planner) by 5/12/00.
11. All members of the management staff have position descriptions and objectives defined for next fiscal year (H. Caring).	15. G. Moore: Develop draft management staff position descriptions for CEO review by 5/15/00.

cussed earlier, the action plan for a given planning year is never completed; new action items
will always surface as you work toward achieving the objective.

As another example, for Objective 8,
expanded office space, Action Item 12 is to
make contact with a realtor. When this is completed, a following action item might be to view
some properties or gather information on potential properties for consideration. Again, the next
action item to achieve a particular objective is
shown, in contrast to describing all necessary
action items at one time.

Action items clearly describe the most basic
activities that must be accomplished in order to
achieve the all-important annual objectives.

Action Items Stemming from Issues

The action plan is where you will address each
issue you identified in Chapters 4 and 5 (Exercise 40). Refer to your Major Issues and
Approaches for Resolution document. Review
each issue and related issue-resolution
approach. You will describe the near-term
actions (next 30 to 45 days) you will put in
place to begin to address each issue you have
identified.

Table 8.11 provides examples of five previously stated issues and issue-response options.
Example action items are also shown, which are

EXERCISE 40: DEVELOP YOUR ACTION PLAN

For each annual objective you developed in your business plan, now
identify the action items you (or perhaps others) will accomplish in
the next 30 to 45 days to initiate the eventual realization of the
objectives. Also, review the list of issues and issue responses you
developed earlier. You may have defined annual objectives stemming
from several of these issues in Exercise 39. Each of these objectives
should have an associated action item. In addition, you need to
define action items for those issues that you did not assign an annual
objective. In other words, each issue-resolution approach you defined
earlier requires a defined action item. Based on the examples shown
in Tables 8.10 and 8.11, document your action plan in your business
plan (see Appendix B).

TABLE 8.11 EXAMPLES OF ISSUES AND RELATED ACTION ITEMS

Issue 1.   We lack sufficient business development (sales) staff.

Selected Response Option	Action Items
If affordable, hire additional sales-people. If not, consider reducing costs in other areas to make funds available.	P. Jones: Prepare and place news-paper ad by 4/17. D. Dawkins: Contact W. Lake re possible hire by 4/21.

Issue 2.   We are not winning our share of competitive proposals; we lack proposal preparation skills, resources, systems, and methodologies.

Selected Response Option	Action Items
Review your business development processes (identification, qualification, pursuit, and capture)—identify and address faults hindering your proposal success. If affordable, hire personnel or re-ain consultants with proposal writing skills.	T. Pres: Interview S. Sharp (consultant) re a survey of our business development process by 4/21.

Issue 3.   We don't sufficiently train our management and staff.

Selected Response Option	Action Items
Implement an employee-training program.	J. Lechter: Survey employees to identify training needs and brief T. Boss by 5/15. J. Lechter: Gather info re training companies by 5/15.

Issue 4.   We lack a structured management organization, authorities, reporting mechanisms; no clear picture of the organization and lines of authority; who's in charge?

Selected Response Option	Action Items
Prepare management position descriptions describing roles, responsibilities, and authorities—include objectives defined in your business plan. Develop and distribute an organization chart.	F. Smith: Gather format for position descriptions and brief T. Boss by 5/2. T. Boss: Develop company organization chart with brief description of roles by 5/2.

Issue 5.   We need to develop budgets and rates and a system to track them.

Selected Response Option	Action Items
Develop a budget and manage it through regularly scheduled reviews. Retain an expert to support the development of the budget.	J. Lechter: Contact J. Numbers (CPA) re a financial system audit by 4/19.

the first steps toward implementing the issue responses. Again, each action item shows what's going to be accomplished in the near-term, who's responsible for doing it, and the action item's completion date.

These examples of action items stemming from the selected responses provide an indication of how you will develop your own set of action items to address your own issues.

WHAT YOUR ACTION PLAN ACHIEVES

Your action plan puts you on the road toward achieving your annual objectives and addressing the issues your company is facing. These near-term activities clearly identify who's responsible for achieving certain results in a specified time-frame. This last element of your business plan is highly critical and must be vigorously acted on by the entire management team.

END POINT

With the development of the tactical elements of your business plan (your annual objectives and action plan), you have now completed the first two steps of the planning process—*defining your issues* and *developing your plan.* The final step is to *manage the plan* you have just completed. Part 4 describes the process you should incorporate in the running of your business to ensure that you appropriately manage your business plan to success.

Manage the Plan

Lots of folks confuse bad management with destiny.
—Ken Hubbard

This part describes Step 3 of the planning process—managing the plan. Three chapters provide you with an effective approach to managing your business plan to success.

Chapter 9: Take Action presents recommendations for managing the implementation of your business plan. Regularly scheduled reviews of your action plan and your progress toward achieving your annual objectives (see Chapter 8) are described. A package to support you in conducting reviews of your progress toward meeting your annual objectives is also presented, along with a discussion of the planning cycle—the timeframe for developing next year's plan.

Chapter 10: Activities to Support You in Taking Action describes three activities to be undertaken immediately following completion of the business plan—review and finalize the plan, hold a planning session (if you have a management staff), and share the plan with your employees. Mini–implementation plans, which are developed by the champions of each annual objective and involve planning the approach for achieving each annual objective, are described.

In addition, a discussion of management by objectives is presented, along with recommendations for holding regularly scheduled staff meetings.

Chapter 11: Business Planning in Larger Organizations is directed at those companies that are large enough to involve others in the planning process. Tips are presented for holding the session, determining who should be invited, meeting logistics, and setting the agenda, and recommended preparatory activities for the session are presented.

Take Action
Implement Your
Business Plan

The fundamental qualities for good execution of a plan is first; intelligence; then discernment and judgement, which enable one to recognize the best method as to attain it; the singleness of purpose; and lastly, . . . stubborn will.

—Ferdinand Foch

The third and final step of the planning process is to *manage the plan* to success. The literature is replete with the call to business owners and managers to implement the business plan you have developed. Recall the citation in Chapter 1 of Nolan, Goodstein, and Pfeiffer's *Plan or Die!*, where the authors stated that "strategic planning and strategic management (the day-to-day implementation of the strategic plan) are the two most important, never-ending jobs of management, especially top management."[1]

Recall also Covey's counsel, presented in Chapter 1, that it is critical to spend time doing those "not urgent but important" things.[2] This is where effort must be expended to implement the business plan you have just developed.

Your plan won't happen by itself. Putting the plan you have just developed aside and opening it up on the last day of your fiscal year to see how you did robs you of the opportunity to take charge of your company's future. You need to undertake and complete the necessary actions to meet your annual objectives. Recall from Chapter 1 that one reason business plans fail is that there is no *management process* in place to support plan implementation. The process described in this chapter presents a methodology for managing your plan to success.

 **MANAGING THE PLAN TO SUCCESS**

In Chapter 7 you developed your vision statement, mission statement, and five-year goals, which comprise the strategies for making your business a success. These three strategic elements of the plan make up the road map you decided to use to take this company of yours where you want it to be. The strategy serves to lay the baseline for the two tactical elements of the plan you developed in Chapter 8, the annual objectives and the action plan—the vehicles for "getting there."

As shown in Figure 9.1, the annual objectives and action plan are the elements of your business plan that you must manage. In the end, they are the crucial steps that must be achieved in the near term. The only purpose of the broader strategy you developed in Chapter 7 is to lend a direction to your near-term objectives and actions.

Referring to Figure 9.1, managing the plan involves holding management reviews, through-

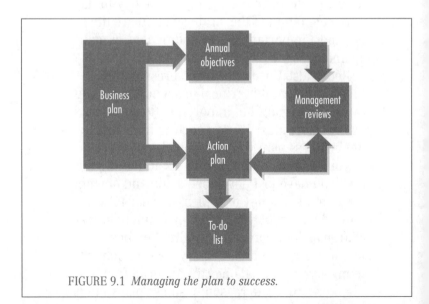

FIGURE 9.1 *Managing the plan to success.*

out the year, of your progress toward both achieving your annual objectives and implementing your action plan. Referring to Ferdinand Foch's quote at the beginning of the chapter, even with everything else in place, it still requires "stubborn will" to successfully implement your business plan.

KEY CONCEPT HOLDING ACTION PLAN REVIEWS

You need management reviews of your progress toward completing the action items defined in your action plan. These reviews should be held on a regular basis; at least every one or two weeks (Exercise 41). For small companies, this review activity should take only 5 or 10 minutes. For larger companies where a management team is involved, consider holding these reviews as part of your staff meetings. In this case, the review should not last more than 10 to 15 minutes. Chapter 10 says more about staff meetings.

Whether you hold the action plan review weekly or every other week, select a day and time that's most convenient for the team (e.g., every Monday at 9 A.M.), and stick to it. If one or two members of the senior team can't be present, hold the meeting anyway, and meet with those who could not attend at a later time.

KEY CONCEPT Updating the Action Plan

The purpose of the action plan review is to go over the status of the business plan action items, eliminate those items that have been completed, and add new action items to continue the pursuit of each annual objective.

As an example of updating the action plan, refer back to Table 8.10, where the first example action item was for T. Smith to develop a list of Fortune 500 companies with headquarters in the Boston area. This action item supported the annual objective of securing $2 million in revenues from Fortune 500 companies. During the review of the Action Plan, if this action item has been completed, the appropriate question is what the next action item is. It may be for

T. Smith or somebody else to contact those candidate clients with the intention of setting up a meeting; or perhaps to develop a letter, including company information, to be sent to those candidates after an initial contact call. Assume that as the result of the first action item, 25 candidate companies have been identified. The next action item might be for T. Smith to contact all 25 candidate Fortune 500 companies by November 15 to set up a meeting to introduce the company. Following action items might include conducting specific introductory meetings or making invitations to the potential clients to visit the company for a presentation and a tour of its facility. Based on this example, it can be seen how the follow-up action items keep you on the path of striving to attain the $2-million annual objective.

 ## The Action Plan Is Never Completed

Your action plan isn't finished until each annual objective is achieved. The action items define the next activities to be completed in support of achieving (or exceeding) your annual objectives. I have had clients tell me soon after their plan was developed that they have completed all their action items. My response is always that they may have completed the initial action items, but they never asked what's next. With a few exceptions, every annual objective in the plan should have action items until the objective is achieved. In some cases, actions for selected objectives might be put off until a later date, for example, hiring a director of marketing and sales in the third quarter.

 ## Be Diligent in Completing Action Items

If an action item is not completed on schedule, inquire as to why and then select a new completion date with the commitment from the person responsible (it may be you) for getting it done. Not all action items will be completed on time, but most should be. To be successful, you and, if applicable, your senior staff need to commit to accomplishing these critical action items. Remember, getting these important things accomplished has big payoffs in the end, such as meeting your annual objectives, having a good year, and being on the way toward eventually achieving your vision of your organization.

Don't Maintain Two To-Do Lists

If you get your management staff involved in the plan, each manager will have responsibility for achieving certain objectives, and their action items should be added to their own to-do lists. I have seen too many cases where the CEO and the senior management team maintain two to-do lists: The first is a list they normally use to manage their time and run the business, and the second is their business plan action item list. This approach will surely set the stage for ushering in a key reason that business plans fail, as stated in Chapter 1: The plan action items lack priority. With two lists, you create the opportunity to do the planning action items later, when things lighten up— a sure-fire recipe for ensuring that the action items won't get done.

Don't Get Bogged Down in Day-to-Day Details

The action plan reviews should not include ordinary day-to-day business activities such as closing a sale, ordering inventory, or getting payroll out. This will bog down the review session. Focus on those necessary activities that support the achievement of your annual objectives.

EXERCISE 41: DEFINE YOUR ACTION PLAN REVIEW DATES

Select which days of the month (e.g., first and third Mondays for semimonthly reviews or every Friday for weekly reviews) and the time of day when you will hold your action plan reviews. Give yourself an action item to hold your first action plan review. Enter the date and time in your business plan's action plan (see Appendix B).

HOLDING PROGRESS REVIEWS ON YOUR ANNUAL OBJECTIVES

You need to hold management reviews of progress toward achieving your annual objectives on a regular basis. Holding monthly reviews provides you (and your management team) 11 opportunities during the year to provide midcourse corrections to keep the corporate ship on course toward achieving your annual objectives.

Select a time of the month and time of the day when you will review your progress towards meeting your annual objectives (Exercise 42). Select a day of the month when your financials for the previous month are available. As an example, if you close your books on the 15th, pick a day in the third week of the month to hold these reviews. If you are the only one directly involved in attaining these objectives, this review should only take 10 or 15 minutes. For larger companies where your senior managers have responsibility to meet certain annual objectives, select a day and time convenient for the team; the review should not last more than an hour.

EXERCISE 42: DEFINE YOUR ANNUAL OBJECTIVES REVIEW DATES

Select the day of the month (e.g., the third Monday) and the time of day when you will hold your annual objectives reviews; hold your first monthly annual objectives review within 30 days of finalizing your business plan. Document this action item in the action plan portion of your business plan (see Appendix B).

DEFINING NEW ACTION ITEMS

When reviewing your progress on your annual objectives, if you (or a senior staff member) are on target for a particular objective, make sure to acknowledge the progress—either to yourself or to the member of your management team who is the objective's champion. Use this opportunity to update the action plan to include your next steps to continue your progress toward attaining the objective.

If you (or a senior staff member) are not on target for a particular objective, it is imperative (as portrayed in Figure 9.1 as the double arrow between management reviews and the action plan) to define *new* action items to get back on target. This is perhaps the most important activity in these reviews. It provides the opportunity to determine the necessary actions to get your plan back on track.

DEVELOPING AN ANNUAL OBJECTIVES REVIEW PACKAGE

Prepare a review package that presents each objective and the status of its achievement (Exercise 43). This package will make your progress, or lack of progress, highly visible.

For quantitative objectives such as revenue, profit, client retention rate, employee retention rate, customer satisfaction percentage, and so on, use charts and graphs. For more qualitative objectives such as having a comprehensive employee professional development program in place or submitting three proposals with a value greater than $5 million, use a simple graphic showing the objective and note its status in one or two sentences.

EXERCISE 43: PREPARE YOUR ANNUAL OBJECTIVE REVIEW PACKAGE

Prepare an annual objectives review package for your business plan using the format suggested in Appendix D. Document this action item in the action plan portion of your business plan (see Appendix B).

Quantitative Objectives

An example of a chart reflecting the status of a quantitative objective is presented in Figure 9.2. This shows the progress of the Waste/Recycling Commercial Division's annual revenue objective of $2.5 million. As indicated, the objective is shown as a solid line over the company's fiscal year—in this case, the calendar year. In addition, the actual revenue of $1.1 million to date (assuming the company last closed its books in June) is shown as a dotted line. Finally, a

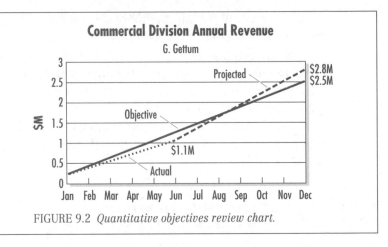

FIGURE 9.2 *Quantitative objectives review chart.*

$2.8-million projection of revenues through the remainder of the fiscal year is shown as a dashed line. Reviewing progress toward achieving quantitative objectives in this manner allows one to quickly determine whether an objective is on track or not. Note that the name of the person responsible for achieving Commercial Division's revenue objective—G. Gettum, the objective's champion—is also shown in the chart.

Qualitative Objectives

An example of a chart reflecting the status of a qualitative objective is presented in Figure 9.3. This shows the progress of the CEO in visiting clients twice a year in order to determine client satisfaction. The objective (CEO visits client sites at least twice a year) is clearly stated, as well as the status of achieving this objective (visited all

---

Client Satisfaction

C. Boss

- CEO visits client sites at least twice a year.
- Status: Visited all major clients in February and setting up visits for September.

FIGURE 9.3 *Qualitative objectives review chart.*

major clients in February and setting up visits for September). This way, it's easy to see whether an objective is on track or not and who is responsible for achieving this objective (C. Boss). A complete annual objectives review package is presented in Appendix D for the sample business plan described in Appendix C.

THE PLANNING CYCLE

KEY CONCEPT

The plan you have just completed needs to be revisited prior to going into your next fiscal year. In reviewing your business plan, you will review your vision statement, mission statement, and five-year goals and make any necessary changes. You will then develop a new set of annual objectives for the coming year and develop a new action plan that supports your new annual objectives. Revisiting your business plan each year is the basis for your continued pursuit of attaining the company you described in your mission statement.

END POINT

Regularly scheduled action plan and annual objectives reviews are a wise investment toward achieving your annual objectives. When you complete your action items and are on track toward meeting your annual objectives, you are on a course toward having a good year, meeting your five-year goals, and eventually making your mission statement a reality. The time required to conduct these reviews is less than two hours a month. This is a small investment of time to accomplish these important business items, and it greatly increases your chances of successfully implementing your business plan.

You are now equipped with a methodology for managing the plan's implementation. Referring to Ken Hubbard's quote at the beginning of Part 4, putting this plan-management process in place will help to ensure that you do not confuse bad management with destiny. Chapter 10 presents several additional recommendations to support the implementation of your business plan.

10

Activities to Support You in Taking Action

Chapter 9 describes a methodology for managing your business plan to success by incorporating regularly scheduled reviews and preparing a prescribed review package. This chapter presents a number of activities you should undertake following completion of your business plan to support the plan's implementation. These include reviewing and finalizing the plan, holding a planning session (for larger companies), and sharing the plan with your employees. Additional suggestions include preparing mini–implementation plans, managing by objectives, and holding regularly scheduled staff meetings.

FIRST STEPS TOWARD IMPLEMENTING YOUR PLAN

There are three initial steps you should take following completion of your business plan: (1) review and finalize the plan, (2) hold a planning session, and (3) share the plan. These are described following.

Review and Finalize the Plan

Take some time, say a week, for all planning participants to review the plan you have just completed and make any necessary changes. If you are a small company, have your mentors (e.g., accountant, lawyer, and banker) and key employees review the plan and provide you with input for your finalization of the plan. Set a target of completing the business plan within 2 weeks of its initial development.

Hold a Planning Session

For larger companies, holding a planning session with senior line and staff managers or advisors will provide valuable input on your plan's strategy and tactics. In addition, gathering their input enables them to buy into the plan and take on responsibility for supporting the plan's implementation. Make them part of your plan and active participants in helping to achieve your vision. Chapter 11 offers guidance in holding this planning session.

Share the Plan

Whether you manage a large company or a small one, share the plan with all of your employees. It will provide them with a strong message that you have your act together, you know where you are going, and you know how to get there. It will also give them an insight as to how they can support the achievement of the stated objectives. Consider holding quarterly meetings so you can report on the plan's progress. For companies with several geographic locations, arrange visits to brief the teams in the field.

 **PREPARING MINI–IMPLEMENTATION PLANS**

As a first step toward implementing your plan, develop mini–implementation plans. Each of these one-page miniplans lays out your strategy and actions for achieving each of the business plan's annual objectives. Figure 10.1 presents an example of a mini–implementation plan for achieving 95 percent customer satisfaction. As illustrated, seven activities or tasks are identified to achieve the objective, along with projected

Mini–Implementation Plan

Name: T. Smith

Objective: 95% client satisfaction, as evidenced by survey

Planned activities and completion dates

Activity	Date
1. Develop project management quality guidelines and present to CEO and staff.	3/4
2. Develop project plan format and ensure all projects begin with a completed and approved project plan.	4/8
3. Set dates and meet with clients quarterly to determine their level of satisfaction.	Each quarter
4. Finalize client survey form.	4/15
5. Develop suggested client visit schedule for CEO.	4/15
6. Have CEO conduct visits and survey current clients.	5/15
7. Get CEO's survey feedback and take any necessary follow-up actions.	6/1

Required Resources
M. Jones: Review and comments on project plan format and client Survey form.
B. Boss: Perform client visits.
Transportation and per-diem, $750.

FIGURE 10.1 *Example of a mini–implementation plan.*

completion dates. In addition, the necessary resources to achieve the objective are presented.

The champions of each annual objective should complete these mini–implementation plans and, if applicable, present them to the management team for review and comment within several weeks of the plan's finalization.

Referring to Figure 10.1, the combination of the seven tasks leads up to achievement of the stated objective. Mini–implementation plans set the stage for moving forward to address each annual objective in your business plan.

 **MANAGING BY OBJECTIVES**

For companies large enough to have a management team, a major advantage of getting your senior staff involved in the business-planning activity is that it enables them to become champions of and accountable for achieving specific objectives. Because these objectives are measurable, you have an excellent basis for effectively evaluating your management team's performance at year-end. This approach is becoming more and more popular in a large number of companies and is called *management by objectives.* In fact, establishing year-end objectives, managing progress, and coaching champions throughout the year is taking place at all levels of these forward-thinking companies, from senior managers to front-line workers. The days of giving all employees a fixed percentage raise at year-end are gone. In today's business environment, you need to create incentives for your employees and pay only for performance.

Consider offering your senior management team a management-by-objectives incentive compensation program this year and moving it down your organization in following years. This approach can go a long way toward addressing the management and personnel issues discussed in Chapter 4 while creating a more effective management organization.

HOLDING REGULARLY SCHEDULED STAFF MEETINGS

Holding weekly staff meetings is a major step toward creating enhanced communications (and operational effectiveness) within your management team. A sample agenda for a weekly one-hour staff meeting, including a segment for the action plan review, is presented in Figure 10.2.

LMN Corporate Staff Meeting Agenda

9:00 A.M.   President's opening remarks
9:05 A.M.   Major activities, organization
            updates, and major issues
                Marketing and sales
                Operations
                Finance
                Human resources
9:45 A.M.   Review of action plan
9:55 A.M.   Closing remarks
10:00 A.M. Adjourn

FIGURE 10.2 *Sample staff meeting agenda.*

Referring to Figure 10.2, following the president's opening remarks (items he or she wishes to share with the group) the manager of each organization will speak for up to 10 minutes. Significant activities that have occurred in the past week or are scheduled for the near future are covered; any changes in personnel or organization are described; and major issues that need to be shared with the management team are presented. Keep the reporting of day-to-day operational activities separate from the next agenda item, review of the action plan, wherein the status of action items supporting implementation of the business plan will be discussed. Following the action plan review, go around the room to gather any closing remarks prior to adjourning the meeting.

Stick to the regular date and time for these staff meetings. In your absence, appoint another manager to chair the meeting. Many companies do not hold these critical staff meetings and therefore miss the opportunity for the entire management staff to come together on a regular basis. If necessary, use a speakerphone to include managers in the field in the meeting.

END POINT

In closing this chapter, it's important to address the commitment you must make when undertaking the plan-implementation process. You have already made a significant commitment of your time and energy in completing the 43 exercises in this book leading up to the completion and, hopefully, eventual implementation of your business plan.

However, the three-phase approach to business planning is not focused only on developing a document called a business plan. Its focus is the *implementation* of the business plan, which requires an even greater commitment. This is a commitment to manage the plan to success through completing the action items in your action plan and reviewing the progress towards achieving your annual objectives. Incorporating this process into your company and making it the basis for your top-management decision making will set the stage for your future growth and profitability.

Chapter 11 presents recommendations for holding your own planning session in larger companies. It is strongly suggested that you undertake this activity to enroll your management team into the planning process and enlist them in contributing to the future success of the organization.

Business Planning in Larger Organizations

When there is unity there is always victory.
—*Publilius Syros*

 **HOLDING THE PLANNING SESSION**

For larger companies, holding a planning session with senior line and staff managers or advisors is highly recommended. The session provides an opportunity to strengthen your plan based on additional input to the plan's strategy and tactics. In addition, gathering their input enables your staff members to buy into the plan and take on responsibility for supporting the plan's implementation. As an example, your director of marketing and sales should take on marketing and sales objectives; the director of human resources, personnel and compensation objectives; the director of finance, finance and accounting objectives; the directors of your line organizations, revenue and other management objectives; and so on. Make them part of your plan and active participants in helping to achieve your vision.

This chapter focuses on those companies large enough to have a management team involved in the planning process. The size of the staff could range from a single employee with management responsibility to companies consisting of a complete management infrastructure including line and staff managers. The line managers are the revenue generators, with titles such as division director, group leader, production manager, sales manager, and so on. The staff managers support the operating entities of the company, and hold titles such as director of marketing and sales, finance and administration, purchasing, and human resources.

Holding the planning session will involve them in the plan's development and future implementation. This will support the creation of *unity* at the senior levels and hopefully will achieve the *victory* for your organization that Publilius refers to in the opening quote.

For those larger companies that are organized into divisions, groups, profit centers, locations, product lines, and so on, the planning effort should first be undertaken at the company's highest level; based on this corporate plan, each business element should develop its own business plan utilizing the process described in this book.

 **FOUR QUESTIONS TO BE ADDRESSED**

In preparing for the session, there are four questions that need to be addressed:

1. Who should be invited to participate in the planning session?
2. What are the necessary logistics of the planning session?
3. How should we prepare for the planning session?
4. What should the agenda of the planning session be?

Guidelines to these four questions follow.

 **PLANNING SESSION PARTICIPATION**

Key people who should participate in the planning session are the senior line and staff managers of the company, including yourself and possibly other advisors such as your accountant, your banker, or a consultant familiar with the business-planning process. Keep the session manageable by limiting the number of attendees to 8 or 10. In other words, invite your key players—those whom you believe help to shape your company.

⬧KEY⬧ CONCEPT Planning Session Logistics

The planning session should be a one- or two-day session combined with some social activities. If pulling senior staff out of the business during the week presents a significant problem, select a weekend or compromise with a two-day session on a Friday and Saturday.

Hold the session off-site to avoid day-to-day business distractions and to stay focused. Avoid telephones and other interruptions. Select a comfortable hotel meeting room, a conference center, or perhaps your own or a staff member's home. If the meeting is held on a weekend, you could convene in your facility, but I still suggest getting away from the business. Get the team into a fresh environment.

For a one-day session, start the meeting promptly between 8 and 9 A.M. and aim to complete by 5 P.M. Provide a light breakfast, offer midmorning and midafternoon refreshment breaks, and serve lunch in the room. For a two-day session combined with social activities, do your planning in the mornings.

The environment and dress should be casual, relaxed, and conducive to free and open conversation. Throughout the session, use a large easel for capturing the salient points of each discussion item during the session, and hang the written sheets on the walls around the room with masking tape for easy reference.

If you don't bring in a facilitator, you should lead the session. Provide an opportunity for your senior managers to voice their thoughts—get them to freely participate and become part of the plan. That's why you invited them.

⬧KEY⬧ CONCEPT Planning Session Preparation

Preparation is a key to a successful planning session. There are four major elements to successful preparation:

1. Share the front portion of your plan, the strategy, with the planning participants prior to the session.

2. Gather the issues your management team sees as getting in the way of the company's success.

3. Get organized—ensure that all planning participants know what position they're playing in the company.

4. Ensure that the participants come to the session prepared to actively participate and make a contribution.

These four suggestions for planning session preparation are described following.

Share Your Strategy Ahead of Time

Your overall strategy is made up of your vision statement, mission statement, and five-year goals. Share this portion of the plan with your management team prior to the planning session. While you don't want to dictate the plan, as owner or manager you should let your staff know up front what you think the company's direction should be. Also, this enables the strategy-development portion of the plan—the most difficult portion—to be more efficiently completed during the planning session.

Sharing your strategy with your management team can be accomplished in one of two ways. Either brief the group on your preliminary strategy, or provide them with draft copies of your strategy. The former gives the group the opportunity to ask questions and make comments on the proposed direction you are suggesting. Your objective in sharing your preliminary thoughts on a strategy prior to the session, whether face-to-face or by just getting them a copy, is to give them an opportunity to see your road map and your approach to getting the company on the road. Make sure they understand that you don't just expect their mute concurrence. You want and need their inputs—not just to gather their support, but also to provide new or enhanced strategies and supporting tactics. Let your managers know what you are thinking in terms of strategy so they can come to the planning session prepared to either agree with your approach, make some minor suggestions for change, or propose some substantive changes to the strategy.

As an introduction to your strategy presentation, I suggest you provide some background on business planning. Use the material in Chapter 1 as a guide. Share with them that the mission statement is created to respond to the five questions posed in Chapter 7—what business you're in, the benefits of your products and services, what distinguishes you from your competition, your major marketing strategies, and what you're committed to. Mention that the five-year goals stem directly from the mission statement. You might also suggest some reading prior to the planning session. Refer them to this book as well as to others referenced herein.

Gather the Issues

You or someone you designate (perhaps a consultant) should hold one-on-one meetings with all planning participants before the session to gather a consensus of the major issues standing in the way of the company successfully implementing its business plan. Group these issues into the nine categories described in Chapter 3. The first activity in the planning session should be to share these issues with the participants. Responses to these issues will be incorporated during the later development of the tactical portion of the plan— the annual objectives and action plan.

Get Organized

Go into the planning session with an up-to-date organization chart so all team members know what their role is in the company. It is critical that every player knows his or her position. If there are holes in the infrastructure, name an *acting* person or leave the position vacant, acknowledging that it is a position to be filled in the future.

Ensure Presession Assignments

Before the session, you should stress the importance of the meeting to all participants. What meeting could be more important than this? You and your management team are planning the future of the company. This meeting is also an excellent opportunity for team building. If you opt for a two-day session, the social activities (meals, cocktail party, golf or tennis) that make up this event should support this team orientation.

To encourage active participation during the planning session, discuss the agenda with the participants before the meeting. Make sure each participant understands the planning process, the objectives of the session, the fact that you desire feedback on the strategy you presented earlier, and the fact that they are expected to sign up to champion several objectives in support of the plan's implementation. In this regard, I suggest you ask each participant to come to the session prepared to agree with, critique, or expand the strategy (vision, mission statement, and five-year goals). In addition, have them come to the session with annual objectives they are prepared to champion in support of the strategy you have presented.

KEY CONCEPT **Planning Session Agenda**

The agenda for the planning session follows the same business-planning process pictured in Figure 6.1—vision statement, mission statement, five-year goals, annual objectives, and action plan. A suggested one-day agenda with time allocations is presented in Figure 11.1.

A discussion of each agenda item follows.

Introduction to the Session

Welcome the participants and let them know the importance of the planning activity to all concerned. Tell them why they are there and what you would like to get out of the session. Needless to say, the real objective is to have the group jointly develop the organization's business plan and have them all really buy into it by the end of the day. Let them know you are seeking their active participation and that any idea is worthy of being presented—but not all ideas will be accepted. In introducing the session, keep to your 15-minute schedule.

8:00 A.M.	Light breakfast
8:15 A.M.	Introduction (opening remarks, session objectives, and the agenda)
8:30 A.M.	Presentation of the issues
9:15 A.M.	Development of the vision statement
9:30 A.M.	Development of the mission statement
10:30 A.M.	Break
10:45 A.M.	Development of the mission statement (continued)
11:15 A.M.	Development of the five-year goals
12:00	Lunch
12:30 P.M.	Development of the five-year goals (continued)
1:15 P.M.	Development of the annual objectives
2:45 P.M.	Break
3:00 P.M.	Development of the action plan
4:30 P.M.	Plan-management discussion
4:45 P.M.	Closing remarks
5:00 P.M.	Adjourn

FIGURE 11.1 *Sample planning session agenda.*

Presentation of the Issues

Present an overview of the issues that were gathered from the staff survey. Don't spend a lot of time discussing each issue. Read them to the group and ask for questions or comments. You want to make sure that everyone understands each issue, and if a large portion of the group doesn't agree that a particular issue exists, eliminate it. Address only the major issues that more than one or two people raise. If an issue is raised only once, consider it suspect. Refer to the Gathering the Issues section in Chapter 3. Tape a copy of the issues to the wall and let the group know that they will be defining near-term actions and perhaps annual objectives to address each of these issues later in the day.

Vision Statement

If you already have a vision statement on your business cards, stationery, marketing materials, and other documents, use the time to determine if it's still appropriate. You developed a vision statement in Exercise 19. Get the group's reaction. When developing a vision statement from scratch, get input on three or four ideas. Refer to the discussion in Chapter 7 for suggestions on developing a vision statement.

Mission Statement

The vision statement describes your company in several hard-hitting and meaningful words, whereas the mission statement establishes your long-term strategy by describing (in response to the 5 questions posed in Chapter 7) what your company looks like 10 years from now—what business you're in, the benefits of your products and services, what distinguishes you from your competition, your major marketing strategies, and what you're committed to.

Use this time to finalize the mission statement you developed and documented through your responses to the exercises in Chapter 7. Don't forget that the participants' ideas for changing or expanding the mission statement may be worthwhile, but, as discussed earlier, you have the final say. Refer to the discussion in Chapter 7 for suggestions on developing a mission statement.

Five-Year Goals

When developing the five-year goals, start off with the ones you proposed to the group prior to the session. Remind the group that the large majority of these goals stem from your mission statement—see the discussion of five-year goals in Chapter 7. Ensure that every distinct point made in your mission statement has an associated five-year goal. Use this time to allow the group to suggest changes to the goals you presented or to provide suggestions for adding additional goals. Use this time to finalize the five-year goals with the group.

Annual Objectives

In developing the tactical portion of the plan—
the annual objectives and the action plan—
make it a truly interactive (team) undertaking.
When developing annual objectives, consider
those you have already developed, but keep
them in your back pocket. Your team came prepared to suggest annual objectives that they
expect to champion. Get them into the plan, and
ensure that these suggested annual objectives
meet your expectations. For revenue objectives,
meet one-on-one with the champions prior to
the session to agree on those critical numbers.
For developing annual objectives, remind the
group that almost every five-year goal should
have a related annual objective. See the discussion of annual objectives in Chapter 8.

Action Plan

When developing the action plan, ensure that
each annual objective has an associated action
item and that each action item has a description
of what's going to be accomplished, by whom,
and by when—see the action plan portion of
Chapter 8. Also, ensure that each issue discussed earlier in the session is addressed
through an action item. Refer to the issue
responses you developed in Chapters 4 and
5 to support the discussion.

Plan-Management Discussion

Remind the group that planning is a three-step
process—identify the issues, develop the plan,
and manage the plan. It requires their commitment to successfully implementing the plan
through management reviews—see Chapter 9.
Incorporating this process into the company and
making it the basis for your top-management
decision making will set the stage for your
future growth and profitability. Discuss the
dates for your first review meetings on your
action plan and annual objectives.

Your Closing Remarks

In closing the planning session, ask everyone to
get you their final comments on the plan within

a week. Compile all the planning information
(from all those sheets hanging up around the
room) and document and distribute a draft ver-
sion of the plan to the attendees by the next day
or shortly thereafter. Remember that the plan
should be only five or six pages long. Once it is
finalized, brief the plan (no need to include the
action plan) to all your employees. As stated
earlier, it's a morale booster.

Just prior to adjourning, start going around
the room to gather any closing comments (you
go last). I have always found these closing comments to be a real boost to the general good
feeling of the group—"We're organized; we have
a direction, a focus, and a business plan."

END POINT

This chapter presents the approach to holding a
planning session. Who to invite, session logistics, presession preparation, and the agenda are
described. At this point, you have completed
your business plan. You have learned of a
process for managing the plan to success, and
you now have a means for getting your management team involved in the planning process.

Epilogue

Begin with the end in mind.
—*Stephen Covey*

Step 1	Step 2	Step 3
Identify the issues	Develop the plan	Manage the plan

The purpose of this book is to have CEOs and other senior managers understand that to increase the odds of developing and maintaining a successful business, you must define and document the necessary strategies and supporting tactics (the business plan), and you must implement a process in the company to effectively manage the plan to success. It all boils down to Stephen Covey's suggestion to "Begin with the end in mind"[1]—plan your business—which completely supports the thesis that one of the major reasons that businesses are not successful derives from a lack of business planning.

RESPONSE TO BUSINESS PLAN FAILURES

Having the plan alone is not sufficient. Chapter 1 indicated that there are four reasons why companies with a business plan in hand fail to execute their plan:

1. The plan doesn't account for roadblocks (issues) in the way of successful plan implementation.

2. The plan is too limited in scope.

3. There is no management process in place to support plan implementation.

4. The plan action items lack priority.

It should now be clear how the three-step planning process addresses each of these four roadblocks:

1. You developed the *issues* facing your company and approaches to addressing them in Chapters 4 and 5 and included them in your Major Issues and Approaches for Resolution document for later use in developing your business plan.

2. The business plan you developed in Chapters 7 and 8 is *broad in scope,* containing both *strategy* (vision statement, mission statement, and five-year goals) and *tactics* (annual objectives and an action plan).

3. A *management process* for successfully implementing your plan is presented in Chapter 9, and plan-management support systems are presented in Chapter 10.

4. The methodology for ensuring that you effectively deal with the plan's *action items* is described in Chapter 9, as well.

As discussed in Chapter 10, the only remaining roadblock to successfully implementing the plan you have just developed may be how *committed* you are to undertaking the task ahead: implementing your business plan. Recall that planning is a *process* and not just the development of a document. Incorporating this process into your company's operation and making it the basis for your top-management decision making will set the stage for your future growth and profitability. You and, if applicable, your management team must make the commitment to spend the time to address the "important but not urgent" activity of implementing your business plan.

REVIEW OF THE BOOK'S OBJECTIVES

Chapter 1 presented three objectives:

1. Provide you with an understanding of effective business planning and plan implementation techniques

2. Have you develop a documented business plan for your enterprise

3. Prepare you to conduct a planning session in your company or organization in order to involve and enroll others in the plan

In regard to the first objective, the first three parts of the book are devoted to gaining an understanding of effective business planning. Part 4 focuses on plan-implementation techniques. The three-step planning process presented in this book is unique. It includes activities to reduce the barriers to successful implementation through incorporating actions in the plan to address the issues or roadblocks present in your organization. It also encompasses both strategic and tactical elements to ensure that it adequately defines a road map to success and puts in place the vehicle for getting on the road. And finally, it includes a management process for monitoring your progress towards the plan's implementation and incorporating the necessary planning actions into your day-to-day activities.

You accomplished the second objective of developing a documented business plan by completing the 43 exercises presented in Parts 2 through 4. This undertaking resulted in developing your company's vision statement, mission statement, five-year goals, annual objectives, and action plan—your business plan.

The third objective of preparing you to conduct your own planning session was presented in Chapter 11. The planning session's invitation list, logistics, and agenda were described along with suggestions for preparation for the session.

IN CLOSING

I sincerely hope you believe that these three objectives I set out for you to achieve have in fact been accomplished. The true test is that you are glad you did not put this book back on the shelf as I suggested you might in the preface. I am interested in your reaction to this book and am prepared to respond to any questions or suggestions you may have. Please feel free to contact me at the following address:

Philip Walcoff, President
PWI Business Solutions
537 Lakeview Circle
Severna Park, MD 21146

I wish you great success in your business and
your life. In closing, I encourage you to always
reach for the stars in your planning efforts. In
this regard, I want to leave you with these words:

*In the long run men hit only what they aim
at. Therefore, though they should fail
immediately, they had better aim at something high.*

—Henry David Thoreau

Your Major Issues and Approaches for Resolution

In developing your list of issues and approaches for their resolution, refer to the examples presented in Chapters 4 and 5. Try to restrict the number of issues in each category to less than five. Limiting the number enables you to focus on the major issues. If you feel strongly about exceeding the suggested number, by all means, include them in your list of issues to be dealt with.

MARKETING AND SALES

- Major marketing and sales issues—see Exercise 1.
- Response to marketing and sales issues— see Exercise 2.

PERSONNEL AND COMPENSATION

- Major personnel and compensation issues— see Exercise 3.
- Response to personnel and compensation issues—see Exercise 4.

MANAGEMENT AND OPERATIONS

- Major management and operations issues— see Exercise 5.

- Response to management and operations issues—see Exercise 6.

FINANCE AND ADMINISTRATION

- Major finance and administration issues— see Exercise 7.
- Response to finance and administration issues—see Exercise 8.

COMMUNICATIONS

- Major communications issues—see Exercise 9.
- Response to communications issues— see Exercise 10.

CULTURE

- Major culture issues—see Exercise 11.
- Response to culture issues—see Exercise 12.

SYSTEMS & PROCESSES

- Major systems and processes issues—see Exercise 13.
- Response to marketing and sales issues—see Exercise 14.

PLANNING

- Major planning issues—see Exercise 15.
- Response to planning issues—see Exercise 16.

RESOURCES

- Major resources issues—see Exercise 17.
- Response to resources issues—see Exercise 18.

B

Your Business Plan
Putting the Document Together

*(Enter the name
of your company here.)*

Business Plan

(Enter the date here.)

(Enter your vision statement here—see Exercise 19.)

Contents

- Mission Statement

- Five-Year Goals

- Annual Objectives

- Action Plan

Mission Statement

- The mission of (enter your company's name here) is to provide our . . . (see Exercise 20).
- The benefits our customers derive from our products and services are . . . (see Exercise 21).
- What distinguishes (your company name) from our competition is . . . (see Exercise 22).
- Our major marketing strategies are . . . (see Exercise 23).
- We are committed to . . . (see Exercise 24).

Five-Year Goals

1. Five-year revenue goals—see Exercise 25.
2. Five-year profit goals—see Exercise 26.
3. Five-year customer satisfaction goals—see Exercise 27.
4. Five-year competitive distinction goals—see Exercise 28.
5. Five-year strategic marketing goals—see Exercise 29.
6. Five-year employee commitment goals—see Exercise 30.
7. Additional five-year goals—see Exercise 31.

Annual Objectives

1. Annual revenue objectives—see Exercise 32.
2. Annual profit objectives—see Exercise 33.
3. Annual customer satisfaction objectives—see Exercise 34.
4. Annual competitive distinction objectives—see Exercise 35.
5. Annual strategic marketing objectives—see Exercise 36.
6. Annual employee commitment objectives—see Exercise 37.
7. Additional annual objectives—see Exercise 38.
8. Annual objectives stemming from issues—see Exercise 39.

Action Plan

(See Exercise 40.)

Name	Action	Date
Sr Mgmt Team	Review draft business plan and get comments to. . . .	
(President)	Finalize business plan.	
	Hold first staff meeting to review action plan (see Exercise 41).	
	Hold first annual objectives review (see Exercise 42).	
	Complete annual objectives review package (see Exercise 43).	
	Brief plan at all-hands quarterly meeting.	

Sample Business Plan

XYZ Systems, Inc.

Business Plan

March 24, 2000

"Making a World of Difference"

Contents

- Mission Statement

- Five-Year Goals

- FY 2000 Objectives

- Action Plan

XYZ Systems, Inc.

Mission Statement

- The mission of XYZ Systems, Inc., a world-class provider of information technology solutions, is to provide our worldwide government, commercial, and consumer clients with networks, computer system integration, business-process reengineering (BPR), and software development services and products.

- The benefits our clients derive from our products and services are increased productivity, reduced operating costs, improved quality, improved employee morale, and support in carrying out their missions.

- What differentiates us from our competition is our sound financial status, reputation for integrity, penchant for customer satisfaction, strong reputation in the marketplace, demonstrated performance on major programs, tightly focused business units, highly skilled technical staff, continuing investment in IR&D, high degree of executive availability, our willingness to change, and our highly creative solutions.

- Our major marketing strategies are to establish and maintain long-term relationships with our customers and business partners, maintain high visibility in the marketplace, continuously exploit niche markets, make selected acquisitions, maintain a highly professional sales force, and focus on leveraging opportunities.

- We are dedicated to total customer satisfaction, to providing opportunities for professional and financial growth to our employees, and to continued growth and prosperity of the company for our stakeholders.

XYZ Systems, Inc.

Five-Year Goals

1. Revenue—$100 million.
   - Client base
Federal government	$70 million
Commercial	$20 million
State and local government	$10 million
   - Services/products—$50 million/$50 million
   - Organization
Networks	$60 million
CSSD	$20 million
Software development	$15 million
BPR	$5 million

2. Pretax income—9 percent.

3. Achieve a good reputation in the marketplace, as evidenced by being on 10 major prime teams pursuing major ($25-million) programs.

4. Bid 10 major ($25-million) competitive programs as prime contractor.

5. Enter FY 2004 with a backlog of $250 million.

6. Achieve visibility in the marketplace, as evidenced by:
   - Publishing or presenting 10 papers
   - Actively participating in five professional organizations
   - Participating in 10 trade shows

7. Have three new core technology divisions in operation.

8. Acquire two market-niche companies generating $20 million.

9. Achieve a 95 percent customer satisfaction rating as evidenced by customer surveys.

10. Have five major offices in operation.

11. Achieve quality orientation, as evidenced by having all program managers PMI and ISO 9000 certified, and having less than $500,000 (0.5 percent) project overruns.

12. Have employee incentive compensation and career development programs fully operational.

13. Achieve annual employee retention rate greater than 90 percent.

XYZ Systems, Inc.

FY 2000 Objectives

1. Revenues—$20 million (T. Pres)
   - Client base
     Federal government $19,000,000 (J. Smith)
     Commercial $750,000 (W. Jones)
     State and local government $250,000 (L. Miner)
   - Organization
     Software systems $13 million (S. Michaels)
     Installation services $3 million (J. Fitch)
     Product sales $4 million (D. Stephans)
2. Pretax income—11 percent—$2.2 million (T. Pres)
3. Bid 2 major ($10-million) competitive programs (S. Michaels).
4. Publish or present three papers (S. Michaels, J. Fitch, and T. Pres).
5. Define new core technology for 2001 thrust (J. Veep).
6. Identify one potential acquisition (T. Pres).
7. Achieve 90 percent customer satisfaction rating, as evidenced by customer surveys (S. Michaels, J. Fitch, and D. Stephans).
8. Develop quality management program for 2001 implementation (J. Veep).
9. Have program manager training program in place (J. Veep).
10. Achieve annual employee retention rate greater than 85 percent (T. Pres).

XYZ Systems, Inc.

Action Plan

Name	Action	Date
Sr Mgmt Team	Review draft business plan and get comments to B. Bishop.	April 3
T. Pres	Finalize business plan.	April 7
	Hold first staff meeting to review action plan.	April 10
	Hold first annual objectives review.	May 17
	Develop and present recommendations re employee career development program to senior management team.	April 10
	Brief plan at all-hands quarterly meeting.	April 26
	Develop contract person job description.	April 18
S. Michaels	Get T. Pres mini–implementation plans.	April 14
	Develop schedule for customer project reviews.	April 10
	Present trade show plan to T. Pres.	April 21
	Develop software systems 2000 revenue projection.	April 27
	Get J. Fitch ideas for paper to be published.	May 12
J. Fitch	Get T. Pres mini–implementation plans.	April 14
	Develop schedule for customer project reviews.	April 10
	Develop installation services 2000 revenue projection.	April 27
D. Stephans	Get T. Pres mini–implementation plans.	April 14
	Develop schedule for customer project reviews.	April 10
	Develop product sales 2000 revenue projection.	April 27
J. Veep	Get T. Pres mini–implementation plans.	April 14
	Present PM training program outline to senior staff.	April 27

Sample Annual Objectives Review Package

Progress Toward Meeting Annual Objectives

July 12, 2001

XYZ Systems, Inc.

Contents

- Annual Revenues

- Pretax Income

- Bid Large Programs

- Papers

- New Core Technology

- Acquisitions

- Customer Satisfaction

- Project Quality

- Training

- Employee Retention

XYZ Systems, Inc.

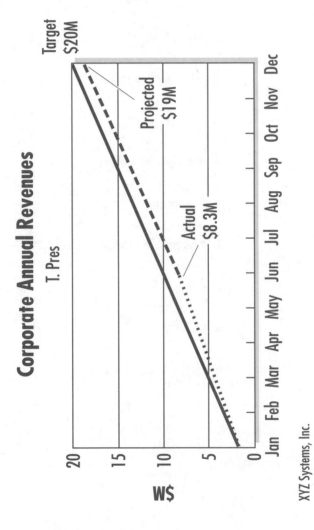

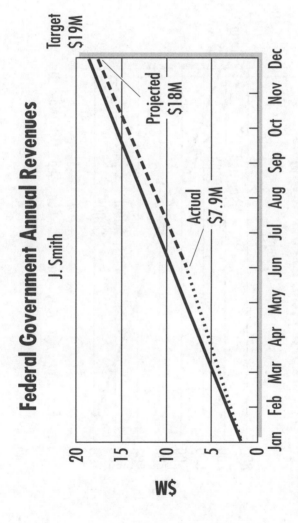

Federal Government Annual Revenues

J. Smith

Target
$19M

Projected
$18M

Actual
$7.9M

Jan Feb Mar Apr May Jun Jul Aug Sep Oct Nov Dec

20
15
10
5
0

W$

XYZ Systems, Inc.

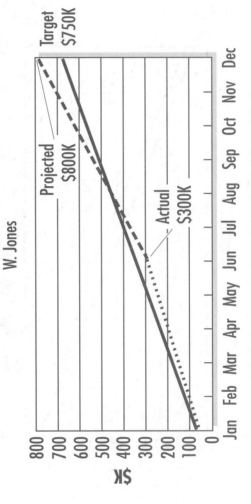

Commercial Annual Revenues

W. Jones

XYZ Systems, Inc.

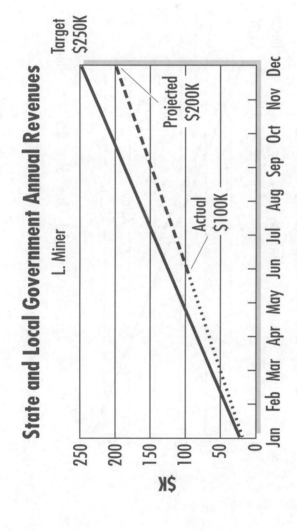

State and Local Government Annual Revenues

L. Miner

Target
$250K

Projected
$200K

Actual
$100K

$K

250
200
150
100
50
0

Jan Feb Mar Apr May Jun Jul Aug Sep Oct Nov Dec

XYZ Systems, Inc.

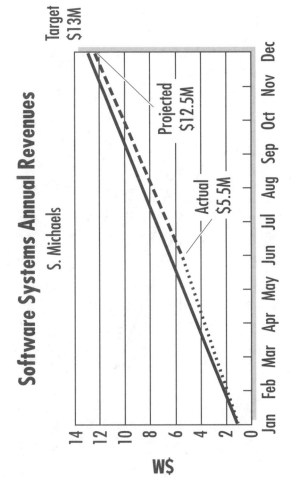

Software Systems Annual Revenues

S. Michaels

XYZ Systems, Inc.

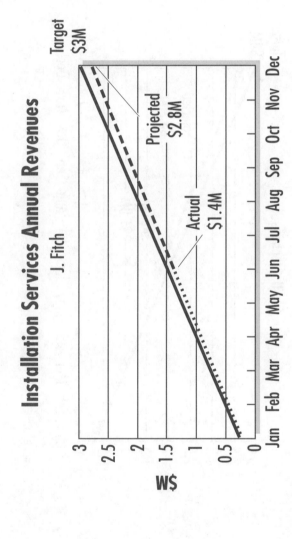

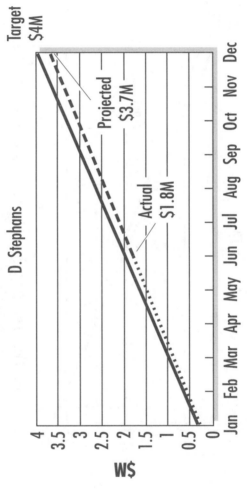

Product Sales Annual Revenues

D. Stephans

Target
$4M

Projected
$3.7M

Actual
$1.8M

XYZ Systems, Inc.

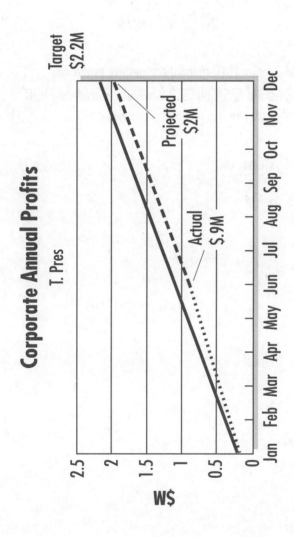

Corporate Annual Profits

T. Pres

Target $2.2M

Projected $2M

Actual $.9M

XYZ Systems, Inc.

Bid Large Programs

S. Michaels

- Bid 2 major ($10-million) competitive programs.
- Status: Bid NASA job ($12.2 million); considering HUD and Army bids.

XYZ Systems, Inc.

Papers

S. Michaels, J. Fitch, and T. Pres

- Publish or present three papers.
- Status:
    S. Michaels presented at AFCEA.
    J. Fitch preparing Army paper.
    T. Pres preparing FedCom paper.

XYZ Systems, Inc.

New Core Technology

J. Veep

- Define new core technology for 2001 thrust.
- Status: Three research programs funded; will select most promising in September.

XYZ Systems, Inc.

Acquisitions

T. Pres

- Identify one potential acquisition.
- Status: Identified three candidates; gathering data.

XYZ Systems, Inc.

Customer Satisfaction

S. Michaels, J. Fitch, and D. Stephans

- Achieve 90 percent customer satisfaction, as evidenced by survey.
- Status: Survey questionnaire in development; will be finalized in July.

XYZ Systems, Inc.

Project Quality

J. Veep

- Develop quality management program for 2001 implementation.
- Status: Survey completed; developing draft policy statement for review in August.

XYZ Systems, Inc.

Training

J. Veep

- Have program manager training program in place.
- Status: Developed content outline; preparing modules; draft curriculum will be ready in October.

XYZ Systems, Inc.

Employee Retention

T. Pres

- Achieve annual employee retention rate greater than 85 percent.
- Status: Currently at 92 percent.

XYZ Systems, Inc.

INTRODUCTION

1. Shailendra Vyakarnam and John W. Lepperd, *Action Plans for the Small Business* (New York: DBM Publishing, 1995), pp. 3–5.

CHAPTER 1

1. *Webster's New World Dictionary* (Englewood Cliffs, N.J.: Prentice Hall, 1986), p. 1088.

2. U.S. Small Business Administration, *The Annual Report on Small Business and Competition* (Washington, D.C.: U.S. Government Printing Office, 1996), pp. 24–25.

3. U.S. Small Business Administration, *Small Business Growth by Major Industry, 1988–1995* (Washington, D.C.: U.S. Government Printing Office, 1998), p. 6.

4. U.S. Small Business Administration, *Annual Report on Small Business and Competition* (1996), p. 226.

5. Joseph R. Mancuso, *How to Write a Winning Business Plan* (New York: Simon & Schuster, 1986), pp. 43–44.

6. Joseph A. Covello and Brian J. Hazelgren, *The Complete Book of Business Plans* Sourcebooks, 1994), p. 2.

7. Dr. Robert Sullivan, *The Small Business Start-Up Guide* (Great Falls, Va.: Information International, 1998), p. 1.

8. Stephen R. Covey, *The 7 Habits of Highly Effective People* (New York: Simon & Schuster, 1990), p. 99.

9. David E. Gumpert, *How to Really Create a Successful Business Plan* (Boston: Goldhirsh Group, 1994), p. 10.

10. *Webster,* pp. 1407, 1448.

11. Timothy Nolan, Leonard Goodstein, and J. William Pfeiffer, *Plan or Die! Ten Keys to Organizational Success* (San Diego, Calif.: Pfeiffer & Company, 1993), p. 121.

12. Covey, pp. 146–154.

13. Ibid.

CHAPTER 3

1. Virginia O'Brien, *The Portable MBA in Business* (New York: John Wiley & Sons, 1996), pp. 13, 24.

CHAPTER 7

1. Joseph R. Mancuso, *How to Start, Finance, and Manage Your Own Small Business* (Englewood Cliffs, N.J.: Prentice Hall, 1984), p. 111.

2. Peter F. Drucker, *Practice of Management* (New York: Harper & Row, 1954), p. 50.

CHAPTER 9

1. Nolan, et al., p. 121.

2. Covey, p. 99.

EPILOGUE

1. Covey, p. 99.